Biblical Reflections on Male Spirituality

Mark G. Boyer

A Liturgical Press Book

THE LITURGICAL PRESS
Collegeville, Minnesota

Cover design by Fred Petters. Carving of St. Philip from Chartres Cathedral, France.

Excerpts are taken from the New American Bible, © 1991, 1986, 1970 by the Confraternity of Christian Doctrine, 3211 Fourth Street N.E., Washington, DC 20017-1194 and are used by license of the copyright holder. All rights reserved.

© 1996 by The Order of St. Benedict, Inc., Collegeville, Minnesota. All rights reserved. No part of this book may be reproduced in any form or by any means, electronic or mechanical, including photocopying, recording, taping, or any retrieval system without the written permission of The Liturgical Press, Collegeville, Minnesota 56321. Printed in the United States of America.

1	2	3	4	5	6	7	8

Library of Congress Cataloging-in-Publication Data

Boyer, Mark G.
    Biblical reflections on male spirituality / Mark G. Boyer.
       p. cm.
    Includes index.
    ISBN 0-8146-2323-9
    1. Men in the Bible—Meditations. 2. Bible. O.T.—Meditations.
3. Men—Religious life—Biblical teaching. 4. Spirituality-
-Christianity—Biblical teaching. 5. Men (Christian theology)-
-Biblical teaching. I. Title.
BS574.5.B69 1996
220.9'2'081—dc20   95–37822
                                                                                                CIP

*Dedicated to
Stephen Witek,
a man-friend on a journey.*

Contents

Introduction   7
Abraham: A Man of Hospitality   9
Isaac: Measuring Up to Dad   12
Jacob: Who's on Top   16
Noah: Build a What?   19
Joseph: Rising to the Top   22
Moses: Who Will Speak?   25
Pharaoh: The Obstinate Leader   28
Aaron: Silent Sacrifice   31
Balaam: Blessing Others   34
Joshua: Finish the Job   37
Gideon: Destroyer of Paganism   39
Samson: Pumping Iron   42
Samuel: A Listener   45
Jonathan: Friend Forever   48
David: Leader of Abandon   52
Solomon: Wise Judge   55
Elijah: Revealer of the True God   58
Elisha: Receiver of the Mantle   62
Tobit: Man Behind the Scenes   65
Judas Maccabeus: Revolter   68

Job: Patient Sufferer   71
Isaiah: Scared of God   74
Jeremiah: Stubborn Is Good   77
Ezekiel: Hungry for the Word   80
Daniel: Keeper of the Lions' Den   83
Hosea: Remarriage   87
Jonah: From the Fish's Perspective   90
John the Baptist: Preacher in the Desert   94
Peter: Flexible and Passionate 97
Paul: Man's Intellectual   100
Jesus Christ: Tragic Hero   103
Index of Scripture Passages   107

Introduction

This is a book about men. While it is about men, particularly biblical men, it is not meant to exclude women. As all of us know, the One God who makes up our spiritual dimension is both male and female. Thus, any treatment of the spirituality of men must acknowledge the feminine aspect. Women-readers who decide to read this book will come face to face with the male aspect of their spirituality. Men-readers will discover their female side as they focus on some of the male characters in the Bible.

As the title of the book indicates, it consists primarily of reflections, which are based on men in the Bible. The book is intended to spark the unique spirituality of men by using biblical characters as models.

There are thirty-one four-part exercises, consisting of a passage from Scripture, a reflection, questions for meditation, and a prayer.

The passage of Scripture illustrates some aspect of the life of a biblical character. The reflection highlights what that aspect is, explores it, and makes connections between the person and men today.

The questions for meditation are designed for personal appropriation of the selection of Scripture and the reflection. A person can use the questions to make his or her own application by thinking about the questions and/or by using them for a journal exercise. Whatever process the individual chooses, he or she will enhance his or her own spirituality.

After finishing the process, a prayer brings the exercise to a close.

Spirituality, the position of openness to the Spirit blowing through a person's life, has a character of its own. This book is an attempt to tap the rich biblical heritage and to make it available to men and women today. Personal appropriation is left to each person's needs and desires.

Because men differ in status—married, single, celibate, father, son, childless—some material in the book will have to be adapted by each male reader for his own use. Likewise, women will have to make necessary adaptations and appropriations for their use of this work.

The author hopes that this book will help men recover their own unique male spirituality and a better understanding of their feminine aspects. He also hopes that in these pages women will find material which will assist their spiritual growth in deepening their understanding of their male dimension and of the spirituality of men in general.

It is the author's wish that both men and women deepen their relationship with God and come to a better understanding of how God's grace is at work in their lives.

Abraham: A Man of Hospitality

Scripture: The LORD appeared to Abraham by the terebinth of Mamre, as he sat in the entrance of his tent, while the day was growing hot. Looking up, he saw three men standing nearby. When he saw them, he ran from the entrance of the tent to greet them; and bowing to the ground, he said: "Sir, if I may ask you this favor, please do not go on past your servant. Let some water be brought, that you may bathe your feet, and then rest yourselves under the tree. Now that you have come this close to your servant, let me bring you a little food, that you may refresh yourselves; and afterward you may go on your way."

"Very well," they replied, "do as you have said."

Abraham hastened into the tent and told Sarah, "Quick, three seahs of fine flour! Knead it and make rolls."

He ran to the herd, picked out a tender, choice steer, and gave it to a servant, who quickly prepared it. Then he got some curds and milk, as well as the steer that had been prepared, and set these before them; and he waited on them under the tree while they ate.

"Where is your wife Sarah?" they asked him. "There in the tent," he replied. One of them said, "I will surely return to you about this time next year, and Sarah will then have a son."

Now Abraham and Sarah were old, advanced in years, and Sarah had stopped having her womanly periods. So Sarah laughed to herself and said, "Now that I am so withered and my husband is so old, am I still to have sexual pleasure?"

But the LORD said to Abraham: "Why did Sarah laugh and say, 'Shall I really bear a child, old as I am?' Is anything too marvelous for the LORD to do? At the appointed time, about this time next year, I will return to you, and Sarah will have a son" (Gen 18:1-14).

Reflection: Among other things, Abraham is remembered for his lavish hospitality. In the heat of the day when everyone should have been taking a nap or resting, Abraham spots three visitors wandering around under the desert sun.

Without asking their names, he begs them to permit him to serve them, to show them hospitality, which in the ancient world meant water to bathe their feet and food to replenish their energy. Abraham welcomes the three strangers into his inner circle of comfort and goes to extremes to show them how extravagantly hospitable he is—a half a bushel of the best of flour to be kneaded into rolls, the best cuts of a slaughtered and tenderized steer, and aged cheese. Abraham spares nothing for these strangers!

Many men have careers in hospitality professions today. They function as stewards on cruise ships, waiters in restaurants, and hosts on airplanes. Their responsibility, while consisting primarily of service to others, is to welcome people in such a manner that they feel comfortable. Sometimes this involves bringing a group of strangers together, while at other times only those who already know each other are involved.

Men show each other hospitality by shaking hands. Two hands extended draw the two men together into each other's inner circle of welcome and comfort. The Western handshake is similar to the Middle East embrace and kiss on each cheek of the face.

In sports events men demonstrate hospitality by big bear hugs in congratulations to a member of the team or as a team hug when winning a tournament. Other signs of hospitality in sports include the touching of hands as a player walks or runs along and the famous pat on the butt from fellow teammates.

Men have a need to both give and to receive hospitality. They show hospitality by welcoming others into their inner zone of comfort. They receive hospitality when others welcome them into their circle of caring.

Abraham represents both aspects of hospitality. As shown above, he welcomed three strangers in an extravagant fashion.

Before his company left, they promised him that his wife Sarah would conceive and bear him the son whom he had long-awaited and hoped for. He received their hospitality, their message of a gift. Even as he offered them comfort, they returned it to him.

Abraham becomes a man's model of hospitality. As the writer of Hebrews exhorts his readers, "Do not neglect hospitality, for through it some have unknowingly entertained angels" (Heb 13:1).

Meditation: Which is easier for you: to give hospitality or to receive it? How are you a person of hospitality? By making a list take inventory of the men and women whom you welcome into your circle of comfort? When you do not show hospitality to others, what is your criteria for judging not to do so?

Prayer: God of Abraham and Sarah, in the person of three strangers you visited the man and woman out of whom you made a great nation. They welcomed you with joy into their inner circle of comfort and ministered to your needs. As a result they received the promise of a son in their golden years. Form me in your ways of hospitality. Enable me to recognize you in the stranger I meet and to receive your blessings. I ask you this through the Lord Jesus Christ, your Son, who lives and reigns with you and the Holy Spirit, one God, for ever and ever. Amen.

Isaac: Measuring Up to Dad

Scripture: . . . God put Abraham to the test. He called to him, "Abraham!"

"Ready!" he replied.

Then God said: "Take your son Isaac, your only one, whom you love, and go to the land of Moriah. There you shall offer him up as a holocaust on a height that I will point out to you."

Early the next morning Abraham saddled his donkey, took with him his son Isaac, and two of his servants as well, and with the wood that he had cut for the holocaust, set out for the place on which God had told him.

On the third day Abraham got sight of the place from afar. Then he said to his servants: "Both of you stay here with the donkey, while the boy and I go on over yonder. We will worship and then come back to you."

Thereupon Abraham took the wood for the holocaust and laid it on his son Isaac's shoulders, while he himself carried the fire and the knife.

As the two walked on together, Isaac spoke to his father Abraham: "Father!" he said.

"Yes, son," he replied.

Isaac continued, "Here are the fire and the wood, but where is the sheep for the holocaust?"

"Son," Abraham answered, "God himself will provide the sheep for the holocaust."

Then the two continued going forward. When they came to the place of which God had told him, Abraham built an altar there and arranged the wood on it. Next he tied up his son Isaac, and put him on top of the wood on the altar. Then he reached out and took the knife to slaughter his son.

But the LORD's messenger called to him from heaven, "Abraham, Abraham!"

"Yes, Lord," he answered.

"Do not lay your hand on the boy," said the messenger. "Do not do the least thing to him. I know now how devoted you are to God, since you did not withhold from me your own beloved son."

As Abraham looked about, he spied a ram caught by its horns in the thicket. So he went and took the ram and offered it up as a holocaust in place of his son.

Again the LORD's messenger called to Abraham from heaven and said, "I swear by myself, declares the LORD, that because you acted as you did in not withholding from me your beloved son, I will bless you abundantly and make your descendants as countless as the stars of the sky and the sands of the seashore; your descendants shall take possession of the gates of their enemies, and in your descendants all the nations of the earth shall find blessing—all this because you obeyed my command" (Gen 22:1-13, 15-18).

Reflection: More often than not, men inherit a dream from their mothers and, especially, their fathers. The dream is what their parents expect them to become, what they expect them to do with their lives. It may also include how they expect them to wear their hair and in what clothes they expect them to dress.

Sometimes the dream is of a better life. Our ancestors, who came from other countries to form the United States of America, did so with the dream of a better life. They worked hard to earn money to buy what they needed and to save for the future. If they didn't attain their goal (and most often they didn't), they passed the torch on to their children, especially the oldest son, in the hope that he would realize their dream some day.

Abraham dreamed of being the father of a great nation. He faced one major problem—a son. Then, when he figured that the miraculous boy was in place and he was ready to hand him the master plan, he heard God's call to give up the boy of his dreams.

But Isaac, too, is a dreamer. His problem is how to measure up to his patriarchal father, who tricks him to take a three-day trip into the wilderness where he will be sacrificed. He recognizes the impossibility of measuring up to his father when he carries his cross of bundled sticks and prepares to be immolated before becoming a burnt offering to God. Isaac, with fear in his eyes, surrenders his dream, his life.

All men sooner or later must surrender both their father's dreams for them and some aspects of their dreams for themselves. They surrender their father's desires when they begin to live their own lives, to decide upon their own careers, to dress the way they please, to wear their hair long or short, no matter what judgment their fathers may make.

They surrender their own dreams when they realize that they will never be able to complete the master plan in one lifetime. The great novel will have to wait for another to write it. The larger house will never be built. Grandchildren will never be seen.

Isaac becomes the model of not being able to measure up to dad. He surrenders to death at the hand of his father. Abraham is ready to give up the dream. But it is at that moment of surrender that both Abraham and Isaac receive in abundance more than they had given up. Abraham receives the son of the promise of countless descendants. Isaac reaches out and embraces the same dream—not because it belongs to his father Abraham—but he desires that it be fulfilled. It is his because it is his and not because it once was passed on to him by his dad.

There is nothing wrong with fathers' dreams for their sons. The father should remember, however, that not all sons will ever own their fathers' dreams. Sometimes, fathers must surrender their dreams for their sons and support their sons' dreams for themselves.

Meditation: What was your father's dream for you? When did you make it your own or reject it? What are your dreams for yourself? What are the dreams which you want to pass on to your children? How willing are they to accept or reject your dreams for them?

Prayer: God of Abraham and Isaac, you instilled in a father and his son the dream of descendants as countless as the stars of the sky and as numerous as the sands of the seashore. Give me wisdom to understand the dreams my father gave to me—both those which I have embraced and those which I have rejected. Guide me in passing on my dreams to my children. Keep alive in me the dream of the kingdom, where you live and reign with your Son, the Lord Jesus Christ, and the Holy Spirit, one God, for ever and ever. Amen.

Jacob: Who's on Top?

Scripture: In the course of that night, . . . Jacob arose, took his two wives, with the two maidservants and his eleven children, and crossed the ford of the Jabbok. After he had taken them across the stream and had brought over all his possessions, Jacob was left there alone.

Then some man wrestled with him until the break of dawn. When the man saw that he could not prevail over him, he struck Jacob's hip at its socket, so that the hip socket was wrenched as they wrestled.

The man then said, "Let me go, for it is daybreak."

But Jacob said, "I will not let you go until you bless me."

"What is your name?" the man asked.

He answered, "Jacob."

Then the man said, "You shall no longer be spoken of as Jacob, but as Israel, because you have contended with divine and human beings and have prevailed."

Jacob then asked him, "Do tell me your name, please."

He answered, "Why should you want to know my name?"

With that, he bade him farewell.

Jacob named the place Peniel, "Because I have seen God face to face," he said, "yet my life has been spared" (Gen 32:23-31).

Reflection: When boys are growing up, they like to tussle with each other. Sometimes they do this spontaneously in play among themselves and roll around on the ground. At other times their horse play is controlled, as in boxing and wrestling matches. No one has to tell a boy that the one who stays on top is the winner. Sitting on the stomach or the back of the opponent or pinning his shoulders to the ground are signs of which boy is stronger.

When boys grow up into men, they continue to tussle. They may fight with fists or gloves or words. Some men arm wrestle. With the appropriate attire others pick up a bat, a racket, a club, or a stick and try to beat the opponent through athletic prowess.

The pen is also used. Writing can become the field or ring where the game is played. Editorials and letters to the editor can serve as the position. Feature length articles can win the fight.

Power, who is on top, is always the issue on the field, on the court, in the rink. Men wrestle with each other to see who is better or best.

Jacob, too, wrestled for power. He didn't at first know who it was, but the man kept him locked in a bout all night. Jacob had already played a game of "skins" with his older brother Esau and won. He figured that whoever this man was with whom he was locked in a tussle, the man would lose. Just as Jacob was ready to make his final move, however, the man hit below the belt, as it were, and dislocated Jacob's hip. But even with this blow, Jacob would not let him go.

With the wisdom of winning which he had acquired, Jacob had no intention of losing. If he couldn't pin the man at the shoulders, then he would nail him with the request for a blessing. Not only did he receive that for which he asked, but he got a new name, which describes him as one who wrestles with God.

All men wrestle with God or with a god. The issue is always power. Men seek power; they want to be on top. In their search for dominance, they ultimately face God, the all-powerful One. Like Jacob, they wrestle with God; sometimes they fight God for years, knowing what God wants of them and refusing to do it.

What all men know is that God always wins. This was the lesson that Jacob had to learn. This is the lesson that is difficult for men to learn. To acknowledge that God is all-powerful is to concede, to end up on the bottom when the tussle is over.

However, God is not a sore winner. God always leaves behind a revelation, a gift, a consolation prize. For Jacob it was a new name, and, ultimately, becoming the father of the twelve tribes who inherited the promised land. Likewise, today, God continues to offer gifts to those who tussle with God, if they recognize with whom they have wrestled.

Meditation: In what types of tussling did you engage as a boy? In what types of tussling do you engage now as a man? How have you wrestled, or are you in the process of wrestling, with God? Who won? What consolation prize did you receive from God?

Prayer: God of Jacob, all through the night you wrestled with the man whose twelve sons would inherit the land you promised. You gave him the gift of a new name, which forever reminds me that he saw you face to face. Give me a greater respect for your power as I stand with empty hands to receive your blessings. All-powerful Father, I ask you this through your Son, the Lord Jesus Christ, who lives and reigns with you and the Holy Spirit, one God, for ever and ever. Amen.

Noah: Build a What?

Scripture: When God saw how corrupt the earth had become, since all mortals led depraved lives on earth, he said to Noah: "I have decided to put an end to all mortals on earth; the earth is full of lawlessness because of them. So I will destroy them and all life on earth."

"Make yourself an ark of gopherwood, put various compartments in it, and cover it inside and out with pitch. Make an opening for daylight in the ark . . . . Put an entrance in the side of the ark, which you shall make with bottom, second and third decks. I, on my part, am about to bring the flood [waters] on the earth, to destroy everywhere all creatures in which there is the breath of life; everything on earth shall perish."

"But with you I will establish my covenant; you and your sons, your wife and your sons' wives, shall go into the ark. Of all other living creatures you shall bring two into the ark, one male and one female, that you may keep them alive with you. Of all kinds of birds, of all kinds of beasts, and of all kinds of creeping things, two of each shall come into the ark with you, to stay alive."

"Moreover, you are to provide yourself with all the food that is to be eaten, and store it away, that it may serve as provision for you and for them."

This Noah did; he carried out all the commands that God gave him.

For forty days and forty nights heavy rain poured down on the earth. As the waters increased, they lifted the ark, so that it rose above the earth. The swelling waters increased greatly, but the ark floated on the surface of the waters.

Gradually the waters receded from the earth.

Then God said to Noah: "Go out of the ark, together with your wife and your sons and your sons' wives. Bring out with you every living thing that is with you—all bodily creatures, be they birds or animals or creeping things of the earth—and let them abound on the earth, breeding and multiplying on it."

God said to Noah and to his sons with him: "See, I am now establishing my covenant with you and your descendants after you and with every living creature that was with you: all the birds, and the various tame and wild animals that were with you and came out of the ark. I will establish my covenant with you, that never again shall all bodily creatures be destroyed by the waters of a flood; there shall not be another flood to devastate the earth."

God added: . . . I set my bow in the clouds to serve as a sign of the covenant between me and the earth. When I bring clouds over the earth, and the bow appears in the clouds, I will recall the covenant I have made between me and you and all living beings . . . (Gen 6:12-14, 16-22; 7:12, 17-18; 8:3, 15-17; 9:8-15).

Reflection: Aren't dads supposed to be always building or making something? Even if they aren't carpenters or mechanics, don't they usually get prodded into building tree houses or doll houses or wagons, and don't they have to fix bicycles, trains, and trucks? If they don't know what they are doing, dads can look foolish.

Think about Noah! As everyone passed along on their way to the grocery store, they asked him what he was building. It didn't look like anything they had seen before. When he told them it was an ark, they just shook their heads, figuring it must be a big toy for one of his grandsons.

Then, when the huge thing was finished, he captured two of every living creature and hauled them into the ark, creating the first zoo in history. What did the neighbors think? What did they say? Such a boat filled with animals made Noah look very stupid.

But Noah is a man of moral courage. His values are those which God approves—especially Noah's faithfulness to God's commands. Fidelity to values is what Noah represents for men today.

It takes a lot of trust to build an ark, especially when a man has never seen one before. Faithfulness to marriage vows and building a family is building what one has never built before. Likewise, remaining true to ordination promises and one's religious congregation's vows can become difficult when a flood of criticism comes along. Getting a project done on time or keeping promises to a group of friends requires a degree of faithfulness. When some friends are cheating, it is easy to try to hide the ark one is building in the back yard.

Perpetuity, however, is God's way. God saved Noah and his family and at least one pair of every living thing to ensure that all would not be destroyed. Those who thought they had the last laugh got swept away by the flood. Those who remained faithful watched the rainbow appear.

When you think that you look foolish attempting to build with moral courage and values, just remember old Noah and the ark in his front yard. While others laughed, he rode on the crests of the waves in his gopherwood boat!

Meditation: When have you looked foolish because of the task you started? How have you maintained your moral courage and values in the face of criticism? What arks have you built? Are they still floating?

Prayer: God of Noah, your wisdom is beyond all our foolishness. When lawlessness had ensnared the earth, you washed it clean with the flood and saved those who had remained faithful to your commands. Wash away my sin. Give me your grace of faithfulness. Help me to build an ark of moral courage and heavenly values. I ask you this in the name of your Son, Jesus Christ, who lives and reigns with you and the Holy Spirit, one God, for ever and ever. Amen.

Joseph: Rising to the Top

Scripture: When Joseph was taken down to Egypt, a certain Egyptian (Potiphar, a courtier of Pharaoh and his chief steward) bought him from the Ishmaelites who had brought him there. But since the LORD was with him, Joseph got on very well and was assigned to the household of his Egyptian master.

When his master saw that the LORD was with him and brought him success in whatever he did he took a liking to Joseph and made him his personal attendant; he put him in charge of his household and entrusted to him all his possessions. From the moment that he put him in charge of his household and all his possessions, the LORD blessed the Egyptian's house for Joseph's sake; in fact, the LORD's blessing was on everything he owned, both inside the house and out.

Having left everything he owned in Joseph's charge, he gave no thought, with Joseph there, to anything but the food he ate (Gen 39:1-6).

Reflection: When faced with a negative situation, more often than not men will complain, but try to find a way out of it. Most men relish the challenge of figuring out how to get out of a rough experience. Calling upon all their creative energies, they plot a course of action and follow it through to achieve the desired end.

Joseph becomes a model of the man who makes the best out of a bad situation. Because his father Jacob likes him best of all of his twelve sons, Joseph is envied by his brothers, who sell him as a slave to a caravan of Ishmaelites on their way to Egypt. After being sold to one of Pharaoh's courtiers, Joseph does not lament the fact that he has become a slave but, rather, demonstrates the kind of stuff of which he is made.

Quickly, he earns the respect and trust of his master, who puts him in charge of his whole household. After serving his master faithfully, Joseph is almost lured into the bed of his master's wife, who tells a lie and has Joseph put in prison.

But does Joseph give up in prison? No! Once again he distinguishes himself with the authorities and is given responsibility for all the prisoners. As he excels in interpreting dreams, he comes to the attention of the Pharaoh, who puts him in charge of the household of the whole nation of Egypt.

During seven years of outstanding harvests, Joseph stores grain for the impending seven years of poor harvests. When the famine finally strikes, Joseph has storage bins ready to feed the hungry. Every negative situation became an opportunity for Joseph to do a good job.

God was with Joseph throughout his ordeals. Today, God is with men when they are faced with problems. God guides them to make the best out of a bad situation. Getting laid off from work is a negative situation which calls forth a lot of creativity from a man. He must begin the search for a new job, while continuing to care for his family, if he has one. He can easily fall into depression, but with God's help he can begin something new. It's not easy, but it is also not impossible.

While driving in Alaska and Yukon Territory, Canada, my Isuzu Trooper II had a flat tire on the Taylor Highway, a gravel road which connects to the Top of the World Highway, another gravel or dirt road leading to Dawson City, Yukon. I was about ninety miles from Dawson City and eighty miles from Tok, Alaska, when the flat occurred. In other words, I was in the middle of nowhere.

After assessing the negative situation, I located the jack, read the owner's manual to find the jack's crank, elevated the wheel, and with great outbursts of energy loosened the lug nuts and removed the flat. Then, I took the spare off of the rear door and put it where the flat had been. After lowering the car onto the spare tire and gathering up the tools I had used, I began to reflect on how I had just made the best out of a bad situation as I continued my trip down the dirt road.

Yes, I was apprehensive. I had no more spare tires, should another tire decide to go flat. Yes, I was alone. But, the strength I needed to get back on the road came to me. At one point I had to use my creative ability, because I could not get the jack under the wheel. But by first putting the jack under the springs, I was able to lift the car enough to get a big rock under the rim of the flat tire, lower the jack and car onto the rock, place the jack under the wheel's axle, and proceed to get the car elevated enough to change the flat. I had not changed a flat tire in about eighteen years.

Daily, men are confronted with employees with whom they must deal, with tasks which must be finished, with problems which come at them from all sides. All of these negative situations offer the possibility to make the most of them. With God's help, success can be attained.

Meditation: What negative situation did you recently encounter and make the best of it? What were the results? How was God at work in the situation, making you prosper?

Prayer: God of Joseph, when this son of Jacob was sold as a slave into Egypt, you did not abandon him but made his work prosper. Because of his creativity, Joseph was able to save the world from famine. When I am faced with negative situations, guide me with the Holy Spirit to a creative solution. Bless me as you blessed Joseph. I ask you this through the Lord Jesus Christ, your Son, who lives and reigns with you and the Holy Spirit, one God, for ever and ever. Amen.

Moses: Who Will Speak?

Scripture: . . . Moses was tending the flock of his father-in-law Jethro, the priest of Midian. Leading the flock across the desert, he came to Horeb, the mountain of God. There an angel of the Lord appeared to him in fire flaming out of a bush. As he looked on, he was surprised to see that the bush, though on fire, was not consumed. So Moses decided, "I must go over to look at this remarkable sight, and see why the bush is not burned."

When the Lord saw him coming over to look at it more closely, God called out to him from the bush, "Moses! Moses!"

He answered, "Here I am."

God said, "Come no nearer! Remove the sandals from your feet, for the place where you stand is holy ground. I am the God of your father," he continued, "the God of Abraham, the God of Isaac, the God of Jacob."

Moses hid his face, for he was afraid to look at God. But the Lord said, "I have witnessed the affliction of my people in Egypt and have heard their cry of complaint against their slave drivers, so I know well what they are suffering. Therefore I have come down to rescue them from the hands of the Egyptians and lead them out of that land into a good and spacious land, a land flowing with milk and honey . . . . Come, now! I will send you to Pharaoh to lead my people, the Israelites, out of Egypt."

Moses, however, said to the Lord, "If you please, Lord, I have never been eloquent, neither in the past, nor recently, nor now that you have spoken to your servant; but I am slow of speech and tongue."

The Lord said to him, "Who gives one man speech and makes another deaf and dumb? Or who gives sight to one and makes another blind? Is it not I, the LORD? Go, then! It is I who will assist you in speaking and will teach you what you are to say."

Yet he insisted, "If you please, Lord, send someone else!"

Then the LORD became angry with Moses and said, "Have you not your brother, Aaron the Levite? I know that he is an eloquent speaker. He shall speak to the people for you: he shall be your spokesman, and you shall be as God to him" (Exod 3:1-8, 10; 4:10-14, 16).

Reflection: Moses is drafted by God for a job which requires that he be able to address a crowd, but Moses is not good at public speaking. So, after some discussion with God about the problem, Aaron is delegated to do the speaking, while Moses does the leading.

Like Moses' felt inability to speak, some men feel like they cannot stand in front of a crowd and talk about a topic, even if they are experts. The gift of public speaking is not given to everyone.

Some roles imply public speaking. The best meetings are those during which all the members contribute. Workshops demand that participants speak. Sometimes men are called upon to give presentations on a specific topic. And there are work and brainstorming sessions, where presenting one's ideas before a group of peers is required.

Moses, it seems, had some type of speech impediment, which gives him a human touch in the book of Exodus. If the great Moses was not able to express himself clearly before a crowd, then men today should not fear either.

Often what is needed is an Aaron. Since Moses could not speak before a group, Aaron did the talking while Moses did the leading. Aaron might take the form of a class or workshop on public speaking. A trusted friend or partner in business might be entrusted with the talking between business and customers. An employee can be entrusted with public relations and take care of all the public speaking that needs to be done.

An assessment of one's personal gifts is all that is needed. Moses was not afraid to point out to God that he was not able to do all that would be required of him as a leader. So, he shared his leadership by delegating to Aaron the task of speaking to the people. Without a loss of self-esteem, men might consider having an Aaron around today.

Meditation: Are you good at public speaking? If so, how? If not, who might function as your Aaron?

Prayer: God of Moses, you called your servant from the sheepfold to be shepherd of your people Israel. Because he could not speak well, you appointed his brother, Aaron, to address the people. Together, these two brothers confronted Pharaoh and led Israel out of slavery to freedom. Give me the right words to speak. I ask this through Jesus Christ, your Son, who lives and reigns with you and the Holy Spirit, one God, for ever and ever. Amen.

Pharaoh: The Obstinate Leader

Scripture: . . . The LORD told Moses, "One more plague will I bring upon Pharaoh and upon Egypt. After that he will let you depart. In fact, he will not merely let you go; he will drive you away. Instruct your people that every man is to ask his neighbor, and every woman her neighbor, for silver and gold articles and for clothing."

The LORD indeed made the Egyptians well-disposed toward the people; Moses himself was very highly regarded by Pharaoh's servants and the people in the land of Egypt.

Moses then said, "Thus says the LORD: At midnight I will go forth through Egypt. Every first-born in this land shall die, from the first-born of Pharaoh on the throne to the first-born of the slave-girl at the handmill, as well as all the first-born of the animals. Then there shall be loud wailing throughout the land of Egypt, such as has never been, nor will ever be again. But among the Israelites and their animals not even a dog shall growl, so that you may know how the LORD distinguishes between the Egyptians and the Israelites. All these servants of yours shall then come down to me, and prostrate before me, they shall beg me, 'Leave us, you and all your followers!' Only then will I depart."

With that he left Pharaoh's presence in hot anger.

The LORD said to Moses, "Pharaoh refuses to listen to you so that my wonders may be multiplied in the land of Egypt."

Thus, although Moses and Aaron performed these various wonders in Pharaoh's presence, the LORD made Pharaoh obstinate, and he would not let the Israelites leave his land (Exod 11:1-10).

Reflection: What is it that makes a man so stubborn? Is it his desire to hold onto whatever power he thinks that he has? Is it his own belief that he must do what he thinks is right for the good of those he leads? Is it an unwillingness to change the course once the journey has begun?

Each man has to answer for his own obstinacy. In many cases, however, stubbornness reflects a man's inability to see more than one perspective—his own. A man can become so determined that he is blind to other solutions to problems he must face and solve.

Pharaoh is such a man. He is determined to keep his slave nation—Israel. Moses' and Aaron's signs and wonders have impressed him, but they have not removed his determination to have his own will done. He needs his slaves to build his cities and to insure the comfortable life which he and his people lead.

Pharaoh has failed to evaluate his options, to look at other approaches which might give Israel some freedom and at the same time keep the nation of slaves. If the Egyptian ruler would have found another away, the whole history of God's chosen people would have been written differently.

There is another important element to consider in an evaluation of Pharaoh's obstinacy; this is God's will. The author of the Book of Exodus makes it clear that he understands Pharaoh's stubbornness to be caused by God. God used Pharaoh to accomplish his purpose—the release of his people.

The same is true in our own day. Through a man's stubbornness God can bring forth good and accomplish God's ways. Because hindsight is always better than foresight, it is difficult to determine when God is engaged in such activity. But who knows—maybe God is at work in the obstinacy of the hierarchy of the Church in not permitting women equal roles with men. Could God not be at work in the stubbornness of some to adapt faith and religion to a modern world? And maybe God works through our own personal blindness to enlighten another in our homes, at work, during play.

No one can be exactly sure how God accomplishes God's will. While Pharaoh failed to consider all his options, God was working to set his people free. Maybe through our own stubbornness today, God is giving freedom to some people.

Meditation: What do you consider your most obstinate behavior? How might God have been at work through you setting another person free and accomplishing God's will?

Prayer: God of Pharaoh, even though the Egyptian ruler did not believe in you, you accomplished your will through him and set free your chosen people, Israel. As I witness your wonders this day, work your will through my stubbornness and reveal yourself through my obstinacy. I ask you this through the Lord Jesus Christ, your Son, who lives and reigns with you and the Holy Spirit, one God, for ever and ever. Amen.

Aaron: Silent Sacrifice

Scripture: The LORD said to Moses, "Take Aaron and his sons, together with the vestments, the anointing oil, the bullock for a sin offering, the two rams, and the basket of unleavened food. Then assemble the whole community at the entrance of the meeting tent."

And Moses did as the LORD had commanded. When the community had assembled at the entrance of the meeting tent, Moses told them what the LORD had ordered to be done. Bringing forward Aaron and his sons, he first washed them with water. Then he put the tunic on Aaron, girded him with the sash, clothed him with the robe, placed the ephod on him, and girded him with the embroidered belt of the ephod, fastening it around him. He then set the breastpiece on him, with the Urim and Thummim in it, and put the miter on his head, attaching the gold plate, the sacred diadem, over the front of the miter, at his forehead, as the LORD had commanded him to do.

Taking the anointing oil, Moses anointed and consecrated the Dwelling, with all that was in it. Then he sprinkled some of this oil seven times on the altar, and anointed the altar, with all its appurtenances, and the laver, with its base, thus consecrating them. He also poured some of the anointing oil on Aaron's head, thus consecrating him.

Moses likewise brought forward Aaron's sons, clothed them with tunics, girded them with sashes, and put turbans on them, as the LORD had commanded him to do.

When he had brought forward the bullock for a sin offering, Aaron and his sons laid their hands on its head. Then Moses slaughtered it, and taking some of its blood, with his finger he put it on the horns around the altar, thus purifying the altar.

He next brought forward the holocaust ram, and Aaron and his sons laid their hands on its head. When he had slaughtered it, Moses splashed its blood on all sides of the altar.

Then he brought forward the second ram, the ordination ram, and Aaron and his sons laid their hands on its head. When he had slaughtered it, Moses took some of its blood and put it on the tip of Aaron's right ear, on the thumb of his right hand, and on the big toe of his right foot. Moses had the sons of Aaron also come forward, and he put some of the blood on the tips of their right ears, on the thumbs of their right hands, and on the big toes of their right feet. The rest of the blood he splashed on the sides of the altar (Lev 8:1-15, 18-19, 22-24).

Reflection: In establishing the cult of sacrifices for the Israelites, Aaron, Moses' brother, and his sons are ordained priests. It is their responsibility to prepare and offer the sacrifices which God legislates.

While ordinary men today are not ordained with such ceremony or with the killing of animals and the pouring out of their blood, every man is a type of priest insofar as he makes many silent sacrifices. Thus, Aaron becomes a model for the man who learns how to sacrifice.

Sacrifice can have a negative connotation. It does entail giving up something. But sacrifice also implies receiving. A man gives up one thing in order to receive something else. And sometimes the "something else" is not equivalent to what was sacrificed, but it is more valuable.

A man might sacrifice a career in order to maintain a value. In the workplace he values honesty, but he sees the system he works within is corrupt. By giving up his career and seeking another job, which will support his value, a man functions as a priest, like Aaron.

Fathers frequently give up many things for their children. A trip is sacrificed for tuition for a college education. A second honeymoon is sacrificed for expensive surgery. A day of rest is sacrificed to spend time helping to work on a school project.

Every time a man sacrifices something of himself, he functions as a priest.

Most of the times these sacrifices are done silently. No one knows that a man wanted to attend the baseball game with his friends. No one will ever find out that dad had planned on spending the whole day on the couch in front of the TV watching football. The child spends his or her college tuition never knowing the sacrifice which saving it entailed.

The sacrificial animals which were used for Aaron's and his sons' ordination as priests signified the type of life that they would be called upon to live. Men today continue in Aaron's line whenever they willingly make their silent sacrifices.

Meditation: What do you consider to be your greatest sacrifice? What value(s) was/were at stake?

Prayer: God of Aaron, you chose one man and his sons to be your priests and to offer acceptable sacrifices to you. The sacrifices they offered were to be mirrors of the lives they led. With your Holy Spirit guide me in making the sacrifices which please you. Help me to follow in the footsteps of your Son, Jesus, a willing sacrifice, who lives and reigns with you and the Holy Spirit, one God, for ever and ever. Amen.

Balaam: Blessing Others

Scripture: . . . God came to Balaam and said, "Who are these men visiting you?"

Balaam answered God, "Balak, son of Zippor, king of Moab, sent me the message: 'This people that came here from Egypt now cover the face of the earth. Please come and lay a curse on them for us; we may then be able to give them battle and drive them out.'"

But God said to Balaam, "Do not go with them and do not curse this people, for they are blessed."

When [Balaam] raised his eyes and saw Israel encamped, tribe by tribe, the spirit of God came upon him, and he gave voice to his oracle:

> The utterance of Balaam, son of Beor,
> the utterance of the man whose eye is true,
> The utterance of one who hears what God says,
> and knows what the Most High knows,
> Of one who sees what the Almighty sees,
> enraptured, and with eyes unveiled:
> How goodly are your tents, O Jacob;
> your encampments, O Israel!
> They are like gardens beside a stream,
> like the cedars planted by the LORD.
> His wells shall yield free-flowing waters,
> he shall have the sea within reach;
> His king shall rise higher than . . .
> and his royalty shall be exalted.

> It is God who brought him out of Egypt,
> a wild bull of towering might.
> He shall devour the nations like grass,
> their bones he shall strip bare.
> He lies crouching like a lion,
> or like a lioness; who shall arouse him?
> Blessed is he who blesses you,
> and cursed is he who curses you!

Balak beat his palms together in a blaze of anger at Balaam and said to him, "It was to curse my foes that I summoned you here; yet three times now you have even blessed them instead! Be off at once, then, to your home. I promised to reward you richly, but the LORD has withheld the reward from you!"

Balaam replied to Balak, "Did I not warn the very messengers whom you sent to me, 'Even if Balak gave me his house full of silver and gold, I could not of my own accord do anything, good or evil, contrary to the command of the LORD'? Whatever the LORD says I must repeat" (Num 22:9-12; 24:2-13).

Reflection: To bless another person means to declare that person worthy of respect. One who blesses another holds the other in esteem and would do nothing to harm him or her.

A husband and wife bless each other with mutual honor and respect as they grow in their marriage covenant. Friends bestow blessings upon each other as they spend time together, talking, laughing, sharing, and playing. When meeting a human being for the first time, we bless him or her with a handshake.

Balaam is brought to curse Israel, whose army is preparing to defeat Moab. But Balaam cannot curse; all he can do is offer a blessing. Three times he tries to curse Israel, and every time he ends up blessing God's chosen people.

Finally, in a fourth blessing, Balaam predicts that Israel will end up defeating Moab and conquer the land. This weaver of oracles, this man of vision, sees what is inevitable and tells the truth.

Balaam is a model of how to approach other people. Today, men are often stressed out. There are so many demands upon them—family, work, play—that they cannot offer blessings. Curses seem to be the first and most available response. Balaam, however, becomes the example of how God works through people to bestow blessings even when they are called upon to curse.

When the car breaks down or the furnace fails to operate or the air conditioning quits on a hot summer's day, a man's first response is to curse the object instead of to bless it. After a little while, however, blessings might be restored. All it takes is a little patience. Remember Balaam?

An argument occurs between husband and wife or between parent and child and curses, spoken or unspoken, are present. If one could just remember Balaam, a blessing might be heaped upon the other person and the argument dissolved.

At work it is easy to curse fellow workers or employers. It is much more difficult to bless them, especially when we are upset by what they have done or failed to do.

What is the bottom line? It is to recognize the innate dignity of every human being with a blessing. If men begin with this point, then blessings and not curses are sure to follow.

Meditation: Whom have you recently blessed instead of cursed? Why did you do so? Whom have you recently cursed instead of blessed? Why did you do so?

Prayer: God of Balaam, when called upon to curse your people, you put words of blessing on the lips of your servant. In moments of anger or stress, help me to remember the dignity of every human being. Give me a spirit of respect for all people that I might leave behind a blessing instead of a curse. Hear my prayer through Jesus Christ, your Son, who lives and reigns with you and the Holy Spirit, one God, for ever and ever. Amen.

Joshua: Finish the Job

Scripture: After Moses, the servant of the LORD, had died, the LORD said to Moses' aide Joshua, son of Nun: "My servant Moses is dead. So prepare to cross the Jordan here, with all the people, into the land I will give the Israelites. As I promised Moses, I will deliver to you every place where you set foot. No one can withstand you while you live. I will be with you as I was with Moses; I will not leave you nor forsake you. Be firm and steadfast, so that you may give this people possession of the land which I swore to their fathers I would give them."

"Above all, be firm and steadfast, taking care to observe the entire law which my servant Moses enjoined on you. Do not swerve from it either to the right or to the left, that you may succeed wherever you go. Keep this book of the law on your lips. Recite it by day and by night, that you may observe carefully all that is written in it; then you will successfully attain your goal. I command you: be firm and steadfast! Do not fear nor be dismayed, for the LORD, your God, is with you wherever you go."

So Joshua commanded the officers of the people: "Go through the camp and instruct the people, 'Prepare your provisions, for three days from now you shall cross the Jordan here, to march in and take possession of the land which the LORD, your God, is giving you'" (Joshua 1:1-3, 5-11).

Reflection: Joshua, who has been Moses' assistant, inherits the job which was entrusted to Moses—the leading of the people into the promised land and their conquest of it. What a major task to inherit from one's predecessor!

Yet, in a manner, every man inherits tasks from his predecessors. Usually, the first task is the burial of his parents. Almost every man must watch his parents grow old and die. His task is to love them through their suffering and to be with them in death. Lovingly disposing of their bodies is his final act of reverence toward them.

In the past one man would inherit his land from his father, who had inherited it from his father. The dream was passed on from father to son of owning a huge farm and tilling the soil and living in a free country.

When people moved from the country into the city, it became the management of a business which a man inherited. His major task became the updating of the business in order to make it more profitable.

Because we are men who dream, we are always, consciously or unconsciously, passing on our uncompleted jobs to our children. We leave something unfinished so that the next generation can carry on the vision.

Sooner or later every man comes to realize that the job he has to do will never be completed in his lifetime. It is at this moment that he looks for ways to pass on the job to his descendants.

Meditation: What major job have you inherited from your predecessors? What major job are you giving to your descendants?

Prayer: God of Joshua, you entrusted the conquest of the promised land to Moses' successor. As he undertook such a major responsibility, you guided him with your law and your promise to be with him. With your Holy Spirit guide me. Help me to accomplish what you have entrusted to me and to pass on the uncompleted job to others. I ask you this through the Lord Jesus Christ, your Son, who lives and reigns with you and the Holy Spirit, one God, for ever and ever. Amen.

Gideon: Destroyer of Paganism

Scripture: The Israelites offended the Lord, who therefore delivered them into the power of Midian for seven years, so that Midian held Israel subject.

Then the angel of the Lord came and sat under the terebinth in Ophrah that belonged to Joash the Abiezrite. While his son Gideon was beating out wheat in the wine press to save it from the Midianites, the angel of the Lord appeared to him and said, "The Lord is with you, O champion!"

"My Lord," Gideon said to him, "If the Lord is with us, why has all this happened to us? Where are his wondrous deeds of which our fathers told us when they said, 'Did not the Lord bring us up from Egypt?' For now the Lord has abandoned us and has delivered us into the power of Midian."

The Lord turned to him and said, "Go with the strength you have and save Israel from the power of Midian. It is I who send you."

But he answered him, "Please, my lord, how can I save Israel? My family is the meanest in Manasseh, and I am the most insignificant in my father's house."

"I shall be with you," the Lord said to him, "And you will cut down Midian to the last man."

. . . The Lord said to him, "Take the seven-year-old spare bullock and destroy your father's altar to Baal and cut down the sacred pole that is by it. You shall build, instead, the proper kind of altar to the Lord, your God, on top of this stronghold. Then take the spare bullock and offer it as a holocaust on the wood from the sacred pole you have cut down. So Gideon took ten of his servants and did as the Lord had commanded him.

The LORD said to Gideon, "You have too many soldiers with you for me to deliver Midian into their power, lest Israel vaunt itself against me and say, 'My own power brought me the victory.'" . . . Gideon . . . kept . . . three hundred men.

Now the camp of Midian was beneath him in the valley.

He divided the three hundred men into three companies, and provided them all with horns and with empty jars and torches inside the jar.

"Watch me and follow my lead," he told them. "I shall go to the edge of the camp, and as I do, you must do also. When I and those with me blow horns, you too must blow horns all around the camp and cry out, 'For the LORD and for Gideon!'"

All three companies blew horns and broke their jars. They all remained standing in place around the camp, while the whole camp fell to running and shouting and fleeing. But the three hundred men kept blowing the horns, and throughout the camp the LORD set the sword of one against another.

The Israelites then said to Gideon, "Rule over us,—you, your son, and your son's son—for you rescued us from the power of Midian."

But Gideon answered them, "I will not rule over you, nor shall my son rule over you. The LORD must rule over you" (Judg 6:1-2, 11-16, 25-27; 7:2, 8, 16-18, 21-22; 8:22-23).

Reflection: Before Gideon could lead Israel to victory over its enemies, he had to destroy the source of Israel's problem—idolatry. A foreign god—Baal—had been adopted by some of the Israelites, including Gideon's father, along with fertility poles. Once these items were out of the way and it was clear that it would be God who would save the people, Gideon was ready to lead the soldiers to victory.

Gideon is the model of a man who recognizes paganism and eliminates it in order to be true to the one, eternal God. Just as foreign gods had been adopted in Israel in days of old, so too many pagan gods have entered our own culture. It takes men like Gideon to recognize these and to guide people back to the true God.

Paganism is found in a culture which worships at the mall. In this place the name of the religion is consumerism. Its slogan is

Gideon: Destroyer Of Paganism

"Shop 'till you drop!" Designer clothes and shoes are the new idols.

Paganism is found in addictions—to drugs, alcohol, sex, TV, whatever. The drug abuser creates a god out of illegal and/or prescription drugs. The alcoholic worships the bottle. The sexually maladjusted individual seeks continual gratification from the god or goddess who will satisfy his or her needs. And the TV is not placed in a prominent position in the house with everyone gathered around it by accident. We worship it from chairs, while prostrating on the floor, or while lying on the couch.

The victory over paganism cannot be achieved by ourselves, but men who recognize how people have fallen into worship of pagan gods are needed to remind us that there is only one God who delivers all people.

With the minimalist of armies, God gave Gideon the victory. Then Gideon, refusing to accept the role of ruler over Israel, reminds the people that God is their ruler. Other gods, such as drugs, alcohol, sex, and TV, cannot rule our lives. We need men who are strong enough to recognize these gods and to lead people to the one, true, and only God.

Meditation: What pagan god have you recently recognized? How did you lead others away from it to God?

Prayer: God of Gideon, you called your servant to destroy pagan gods in your land. Faithful to his role, Gideon led your people to victory and peace. Help me to recognize the false idols in my life and give me the courage to remove them. May I always worship only you, the one, eternal God, who is Father, Son, and Holy Spirit, for ever and ever. Amen.

Samson: Pumping Iron

Scripture: There was a certain man from Zorah, of the clan of the Danites whose name was Manoah. His wife was barren and had borne no children. An angel of the LORD appeared to the woman and said to her, "Though you are barren and have had no children, yet you will conceive and bear a son. Now, then, be careful to take no wine or strong drink and to eat nothing unclean. As for the son you will conceive and bear, no razor shall touch his head, for this boy is to be consecrated to God from the womb. It is he who will begin the deliverance of Israel from the power of the Philistines."

The woman bore a son and named him Samson. The boy grew up and the LORD blessed him . . . .

. . . Samson . . . caught three hundred foxes. Turning them tail to tail, he tied between each pair of tails one of the torches he had at hand. He then kindled the torches and set the foxes loose in the standing grain of the Philistines, thus burning both the shocks and the standing grain, and the vineyards and olive orchards as well.

When the Philistines asked who had done this, they were told, "Samson . . . ."

. . . He fell in love with a woman . . . whose name was Delilah. The lords of the Philistines came to her and said, "Beguile him and find out the secret of his great strength, and how we may overcome and bind him so as to keep him helpless."

So he took her completely into his confidence and told her, "No razor has touched my head, for I have been consecrated to God from my mother's womb. If I am shaved, my strength will leave me, and I shall be as weak as any other man!"

She had him sleep on her lap, and called for a man who shaved off his seven locks of hair. Then she began to mistreat him, for his strength had left him. When she said, "The Philistines are upon you, Samson!", and he woke from his sleep, he thought he could make good his escape . . . . But the Philistines seized him and gouged out his eyes. Then they brought him down to Gaza and bound him with bronze fetters, and he was put to grinding in the prison. But the hair of his head began to grow as soon as it was shaved off.

The lords of the Philistines assembled to offer a great sacrifice to their god . . . . When their spirits were high, they said, "Call Samson that he may amuse us." So they called Samson from the prison, and he played the buffoon before them.

Then they stationed him between the columns [that supported the temple].

Samson cried out to the LORD and said, "O Lord GOD, remember me! Strengthen me, O God, this last time for my two eyes that I may avenge myself once and for all on the Philistines." Samson grasped the two middle columns on which the temple rested and braced himself against them, one at his right hand, the other at his left. And Samson said, "Let me die with the Philistines!"

He pushed hard, and the temple fell upon the lords and all the people who were in it (Judg 13:2-5, 24; 15:4-5; 16:4-5, 17, 19-25, 28-30).

Reflection: Samson is a man of steel both on the outside and on the inside. Besides his obvious physical strength, he is also a man of spiritual strength; he knows from where his power comes.

This is not meant to imply that Samson is not human. He is portrayed as a man who possesses the whole range of human emotions. He falls in love, he gets angry, he kills, he takes revenge on his enemies. In fact, it is Samson's human dimension which makes him admirable and a model for men who pump iron.

Physicality, the way a man looks, is a great consideration by most men today. From their early years in athletics, they are found in gyms and weight rooms pumping iron. Muscles must be firm and pronounced. Broad shoulders and a dark tan make the body look like that of a Greek or Roman god.

Once high school and college days are done, many men join health clubs, where they continue to keep themselves in shape. Eating the right type of foods and maintaining a rigid diet and exercise program can become the new religion for some men.

While the physical dimension is important, Samson reminds us that the spiritual dimension is also important. A certain amount of strength to lift weights can be developed, but spiritual rigor is also needed for a man to be truly rounded.

When Samson was faced with crisis, he usually turned to God. While he was physically strong enough to defeat his enemies, he was aware of his total reliance upon God for the victory. A healthy body that is in shape is but one aspect of the total person. The spiritual dimension cannot be ignored if the individual man is to be complete. In fact the two work together. The physical strength enhances the spiritual strength, and the spiritual strength adds to the physical strength.

Meditation: In which ways are you physically strong? In which ways are you spiritually strong? How are these connected?

Prayer: God of Samson, you made your servant physically strong so that he might defeat the enemies of your chosen people, Israel. However, you also gave him spiritual energy that he might use his strength to accomplish your will. Give me a greater appreciation for both strength of body and spirit. Form me in the image of Jesus Christ, your Son, who lives and reigns with you and the Holy Spirit, one God, for ever and ever. Amen.

Samuel: A Listener

Scripture: During the time young Samuel was minister to the LORD under Eli, a revelation of the LORD was uncommon and vision infrequent. One day Eli was asleep in his usual place. His eyes had lately grown so weak that he could not see. The lamp of God was not yet extinguished, and Samuel was sleeping in the temple of the LORD where the ark of God was. The LORD called to Samuel, who answered, "Here I am."

He ran to Eli and said, "Here I am. You called me."

"I did not call you," Eli said. "Go back to sleep."

So he went back to sleep. Again the LORD called Samuel, who rose and went to Eli. "Here I am," he said. "You called me."

But he answered, "I did not call you, my son. Go back to sleep."

At that time Samuel was not familiar with the LORD, because the LORD had not revealed anything to him as yet. The LORD called Samuel again, for the third time. Getting up and going to Eli, he said, "Here I am. You called me."

Then Eli understood that the LORD was calling the youth. So he said to Samuel, "Go to sleep, and if you are called, reply, 'Speak, LORD, for your servant is listening.'"

When Samuel went to sleep in his place, the LORD came and revealed his presence, calling out as before, "Samuel, Samuel!"

Samuel answered, "Speak, for your servant is listening."

The LORD said to Samuel: "I am about to do something in Israel that will cause the ears of everyone who hears it to ring. On that day I will carry out in full against Eli everything I threatened against his family. I announce to him that I am condemning his family once and for all, because of this crime: though he knew his sons were blaspheming God, he did not reprove them. Therefore, I swear to the family of Eli that no sacrifice or offering will ever expiate its crime."

Samuel then slept until morning, when he got up early and opened the doors of the temple of the LORD. He feared to tell Eli the vision, but Eli called to him, "Samuel, my son!"

He replied, "Here I am."

Then Eli asked, "What did he say to you? Hide nothing from me!"

So Samuel told him everything, and held nothing back.

Eli answered, "He is the LORD. He will do what he judges best" (1 Sam 3:1-18).

Reflection: There is a difference between hearing and listening. We hear a lot during every day, but we listen to little. We hear the wind blowing, motors running, and people talking. However, to most of what we hear we pay no attention. This means that we are not even aware of all the noise which enters into our ears.

Listening implies that we focus our ears on what we are hearing. We might go to a symphony orchestra and focus on the instruments and the notes of a piece by Beethoven. We concentrate on what we are hearing—that is listening.

A counsellor spends most of his or her days listening attentively to what a patient is saying. It is only through intensive listening that the problem can be diagnosed and help offered.

When friends and lovers get together, they engage in listening. Each word of the other is held in reverence and tasted and digested. Through the art of listening people get to know each other.

Listening is tiresome. If you want to be worn out quickly, spend a few hours listening intently to another person. You will come away drained because you invested so much psychic energy into listening to what the other person was saying.

Listening is required of God. Like Samuel, who was taught how to listen by Eli, so men today need to be taught how to listen. In the quiet of the night, Samuel hears God's call. Eli tells him to simply acknowledge that he is present and that he is listening.

This requires that Samuel assume the role of a servant, like Eli had done. It implies that both of these men are dependent upon God to work God's will through them. Even when Eli receives the bad news that his sons will not continue as leaders of Israel, he relies upon God to do what is best.

Listening implies reliance upon God. It is in the quiet of the night or in the silence of a mountain top or the insulation of the forest or the desolation of the desert that a man can listen. God speaks, but the daily hearing does not permit us to listen. So, it is important to find a place where a few moments of listening can be had.

Meditation: To whom did you most recently spend time listening? When did you listen to God? Where is your favorite place for listening?

Prayer: God of Samuel, in the quiet of the night you called your servant. Because Eli had taught him how to listen, you revealed yourself and delivered your message to the one whose words you would make effective for your people, Israel. Guide me to a place of silence that I might listen to you and to others. Send me your Spirit to prepare me to be a listening servant, like Jesus Christ, your Son, who lives and reigns with you and the Holy Spirit, one God, for ever and ever. Amen.

Jonathan: Friend Forever

Scripture: . . . When David returned from slaying the Philistine, Abner took him and presented him to Saul. David was still holding the Philistine's head.

Saul then asked him, "Whose son are you, young man?"

David replied, "I am the son of your servant Jesse of Bethlehem."

[By the time David finished speaking with Saul, Jonathan (Saul's son) had become as fond of David as if his life depended on him; he loved him as he loved himself. Saul laid claim to David that day and did not allow him to return to his father's house. And Jonathan entered into a bond with David, because he loved him as himself.

Jonathan divested himself of the mantle he was wearing and gave it to David, along with his military dress, and his sword, his bow and his belt. David then carried out successfully every mission on which Saul sent him.]

Saul discussed his intention of killing David with his son Jonathan and with all his servants. But Saul's son Jonathan, who was very fond of David, told him: "My father Saul is trying to kill you. Therefore, please be on your guard tomorrow morning; get out of sight and remain in hiding. I, however, will go out and stand beside my father in the countryside where you are, and will speak to him about you. If I learn anything, I will let you know."

Jonathan then spoke well of David to his father Saul, saying to him: "Let not your majesty sin against his servant David, for he has committed no offense against you, but has helped you very much by his deeds. When he took his life in his hands and slew the Philistine, and the LORD brought about a great victory for all Israel through him, you were glad to see it. Why, then, should you become guilty of shedding innocent blood by killing David without cause?"

Saul heeded Jonathan's plea and swore, "As the LORD lives, he shall not be killed."

So Jonathan summoned David and repeated the whole conversation to him. Jonathan then brought David to Saul, and David served him as before.

When war broke out again, David went out to fight against the Philistines and inflicted a great defeat upon them, putting them to flight. Then an evil spirit from the LORD came upon Saul as he was sitting in his house with spear in hand and David was playing the harp nearby. Saul tried to nail David to the wall with the spear, but David eluded Saul, so that the spear struck only the wall, and David got away safe.

David . . . went to Jonathan. "What have I done?" he asked him. "What crime or what offense does your father hold against me that he seeks my life?"

Jonathan answered him: "Heaven forbid that you should die! My father does nothing, great or small, without disclosing it to me. Why, then, should my father conceal this from me? This cannot be so!"

But David replied: "Your father is well aware that I am favored with your friendship, so he has decided, 'Jonathan must not know of this lest he be grieved.' Nevertheless, as the LORD lives and as you live, there is but a step between me and death."

Jonathan then said to David, "I will do whatever you wish."

But Saul was extremely angry with Jonathan and said to him: "Son of a rebellious woman, do I not know that, to your own shame and to the disclosure of your mother's shame, you are the companion of Jesse's son? Why, as long as the son of Jesse lives upon the earth, you cannot make good your claim to the kingship! So send for him, and bring him to me, for he is doomed."

But Jonathan asked his father Saul: "Why should he die? What has he done?"

At this Saul brandished his spear to strike him, and thus Jonathan learned that his father was resolved to kill David.

The next morning Jonathan went out into the field . . . David rose . . . and prostrated himself on the ground three times before Jonathan in homage. They kissed each other and wept aloud together. At length Jonathan said to David, "Go in peace, in keeping with what we two have sworn by the name of the LORD: 'The LORD shall be between you and me, and between your posterity and mine forever.'"

Then David departed on his way, while Jonathan went back into the city (1 Sam 17:55-58; 18:1-5; 19:1-10; 20:1-4, 30-33, 35, 41-42; 21:1).

Reflection: A true friend is a priceless gift. Most men have no more than two or three intimate male friends throughout their lifetimes. And in the homophobic world of today, such a fear of intimacy has developed between men that true and lasting friendships may become a rarity.

Yet, more than ever, a man needs a friend with whom he can share his vulnerability. A man needs another man to whom he can turn in trust and with whom he can share his problems and successes with no false fronts. Since men are usually pitted against each other, vulnerability seldom is seen or expressed. This is why a faithful friend, who can share one's failures, is needed.

Just as men need each other, so do boys need men as mentors. A boy, a potential man, needs to be initiated into the world of men's strengths and weaknesses. Usually, this is accomplished by the boy's grandfather or father, but another man might also be involved in the process.

What are the topics which men share with men and which they share with boys? The most obvious is that of sexuality—a respect for the procreative powers. Men talk about love and its successes and failures. Men share feelings about their jobs and the tension they experience. In athletic competition they pit their physical strength against each other, knowing that there is something about combat on the field or on the court. In the gym and in the locker room, they are able to communicate with each other in a space which is non-threatening to their weaknesses.

Jonathan was David's true friend. Jonathan was worthy of trust. He was selfless, even to the point of sacrificing the kingship, which he would inherit from his father. Jonathan loved David, and David loved Jonathan.

They are able to kiss each other, hug each other, love each other deeply without any sexual overtones. Today, men need the same kind of support from other men. They want to be able to love each other deeply and to share each other's joys and sorrows. They search for a true friend who will share such a relationship with them. They search for a true friend who will not betray their weaknesses.

Meditation: Who are your true friends? Identify what you have shared with each. For what kind of friend are you currently searching?

Prayer: God of Jonathan, you made David's companion a trustworthy friend, one who was truly unselfish in word and in deed. I thank you for the male companions you have given to me. Continue to give me friends with whom I can share my joys and sorrows. I ask you this through the Lord Jesus Christ, your Son, who lives and reigns with you and the Holy Spirit, one God, for ever and ever. Amen.

David: Leader of Abandon

Scripture: All the tribes of Israel came to David in Hebron and said: "Here we are, your bone and your flesh. In days past, when Saul was our king, it was you who led the Israelites out and brought them back. And the LORD said to you, 'You shall shepherd my people Israel and shall be commander of Israel.'"

When all the elders of Israel came to David in Hebron, King David made an agreement with them there before the LORD, and they anointed him king of Israel.

. . . David and all the people who were with him set out . . . to bring up . . . the ark of God, which bears the name of the LORD of hosts enthroned above the cherubim. . . . David went to bring up the ark of God . . . into the City of David amid festivities.

As soon as the bearers of the ark of the LORD had advanced six steps, he sacrificed an ox and a fatling. Then David, girt with a linen apron, came dancing before the LORD with abandon, as he and all the Israelites were bringing up the ark of the LORD with shouts of joy and to the sound of the horn.

The ark of the LORD was brought in and set in its place within the tent David had pitched for it. Then David offered holocausts and peace offerings before the LORD. When he finished making these offerings, he blessed the people in the name of the LORD of hosts. He then distributed among all the people, to each man and each woman in the entire multitude of Israel, a loaf of bread, a cut of roast meat, and a raisin cake. With this, all the people left for their homes.

One evening David rose from his siesta and strolled about on the roof of the palace. From the roof he saw a woman bathing, who was very beautiful. David had inquiries made about the woman and was told, "She is Bathsheba, . . . and wife of . . . Uriah the Hittite."

Then David sent messengers and took her. When she came to him, he had relations with her . . . . She then returned to her house. But the woman had conceived, and sent the information to David, "I am with child" (2 Sam 5:1-3; 6:2, 12-15, 17-19; 11:2-5).

Reflection: David is a mixture of a person of what most men experience themselves to be. He is a warrior, a king, a lover, a sinner, a father. David is like the many facets of a single diamond; while one facet sparkles in the light, another facet is hidden in the darkness. Thus, the best word to describe this man is abandon.

David abandons himself to whatever he is involved. He gets totally absorbed in moving the ark of God to the tent in Jerusalem. With abandon he offers sacrifices to God and dances before the ark. For a man, who is the exalted leader of his people, to strip himself to his underwear and engage in a dance of abandon is unheard of.

In war David abandons himself to the pursuit of victory. He leads Israel to conquer the enemy and establishes the borders of the kingdom as far as the eye can see. No force is too great for David to meet on the field of battle.

As king, David usually prepares all the moves and keeps all under his royal control. The abandon to kingship is ironically compared to David's shepherd status as a youth, during which David surrendered himself to the flock.

David is also a lover, who abandons himself into the arms of his wives and the wife of Uriah, Bathsheba. Such loving results in a child.

David is a sinner. Not only does he lust for and sleep with Bathsheba, but he also plots the death of Uriah, her husband. Once his sin is pointed out to him by Nathan, he repents of his crime.

As a father, David faces problems with his children, especially his son Absalom, who plots his father's defeat. His son Amnon seduces his half-sister Tamar. David's family is filled with problems.

Like David, men today can face their many-faceted lives with abandon. They may not strip down to their underwear and dance in the middle of a street before a church, but they must be warriors, kings, lovers, sinners, and maybe fathers, if they are to survive.

As warriors they fight not on the battlefields of war (although if they are in the armed services, they may do this too) but on the ground of principles and justice. As kings they take great pride in being their own bosses and making decisions.

Men know how to love deeply, both women and other men. They also know their own weaknesses and often fall, not being all they wish they could be.

Some men father children, who call forth new strengths from them. The ideal family life is often shattered by the reality of different people attempting to live together under the same roof.

It is a challenge to keep all of life somewhat together. David is a model of one who tried, of one who represents a mixture of what men are and all of the potential that they possess.

Meditation: When have you experienced yourself in abandon? How are you like David, a warrior, a king, a lover, a sinner, a father?

Prayer: God of David, from the sheepfold you chose the warrior who would be the king of your people Israel. Even when he fell into sin, you did not abandon him, but promised that his kingship would endure for all time. Guide me with your Spirit of abandon that I might be a good warrior, king, and lover. When I sin, help me to know your forgiveness through Jesus Christ, your Son, who lives and reigns with you and the Holy Spirit, one God, for ever and ever. Amen.

Solomon: Wise Judge

Scripture: Solomon loved the LORD, and obeyed the statutes of his father David; yet he offered sacrifice and burned incense on the high places.

The king went to Gibeon to sacrifice there, because that was the most renowned high place. Upon its altar Solomon offered a thousand holocausts. In Gibeon the LORD appeared to Solomon in a dream at night.

God said, "Ask something of me and I will give it to you."

Solomon answered: "You have shown great favor to our servant, my father David, because he behaved faithfully toward you, with justice and an upright heart; and you have continued this great favor toward him, even today, seating a son of his on his throne. O LORD, my God, you have made me, your servant, king to succeed my father David; but I am a mere youth, not knowing at all how to act. I serve you in the midst of the people whom you have chosen, a people so vast that it cannot be numbered or counted. Give your servant, therefore, an understanding heart to judge your people and to distinguish right from wrong. For who is able to govern this vast people of yours?"

The LORD was pleased that Solomon made this request. So God said to him: "Because you have asked for this—not for a long life for yourself, nor for riches, nor for the life of your enemies, but for understanding so that you may know what is right—I do as you requested. I give you a heart so wise and understanding that there has never been anyone like you up to now, and after you there will come no one to equal you. In addition, I give you what you have not asked for, such riches and glory that among kings there is not your like. And if you follow me by keeping my statutes and commandments, as your father David did, I will give you a long life."

When Solomon awoke from his dream, he went to Jerusalem, stood before the ark of the covenant of the LORD, offered holocausts and peace offerings, and gave a banquet for all his servants (1 Kgs 3:3-15).

Reflection: Solomon is a model of wisdom, the ability to make decisions after carefully weighing all the information. As the successor to the kingship of his father, David, Solomon asks God for only the gift of wisdom to govern the people.

Every day men have to make decisions which affect their lives and the lives of others. In the world of business a man may have to decide to buy or sell stocks, which applicants to hire as new employees, what products to buy, and what inventory to eliminate.

Men decide matters at home, maybe in conjunction with a spouse or maybe alone. Should I buy this house? Should I buy this car? How much should I save for my children's college education? How will I get the lawn mowed, attend the children's games, finish a few household projects, and still get some rest this weekend?

Decisions about health must also be made. Men need health care. They need a regular program of exercise and diet. They need time to play and to work out with other men in athletics. A man's social life is part of his over-all health network.

These are only a few of the many areas which require decisions every day. Men are called upon to be wise, to exercise wisdom. It takes practice and skill to make decisions after gathering all the information possible. The truly wise man knows the process and engages in it regularly—that is why he is a man of wisdom!

Meditation: What was the last major decision which you had to make? How did you collect information? How are you wiser because of your decision? With whom did you collaborate?

Prayer: God of Solomon, because the king you had chosen to rule your people did not ask for a long life or riches or the death of his enemies, but for wisdom, you gave him all else besides. With your Holy Spirit make me truly wise. Help me to understand, to collect the information I need, and to proceed with you at my side. I ask you this in the name of Jesus Christ, your Son, who lives and reigns with you and the Holy Spirit, one God, for ever and ever. Amen.

Elijah: Revealer of the True God

Scripture: [Elijah said to Ahab:] ". . . Summon all Israel to me on Mount Carmel, as well as the four hundred and fifty prophets of Baal and the four hundred prophets of Asherah who eat at Jezebel's table."

So Ahab sent to all the Israelites and had the prophets assemble on Mount Carmel.

Elijah appealed to all the people and said, "How long will you straddle the issue? If the LORD is God, follow him; if Baal, follow him."

The people, however, did not answer him. So Elijah said to the people, "I am the only surviving prophet of the LORD, and there are four hundred and fifty prophets of Baal. Give us two young bulls. Let them choose one, cut it into pieces, and place it on the wood, but start no fire. I shall prepare the other and place it on the wood, but shall start no fire. You shall call on your gods, and I will call on the LORD. The God who answers with fire is God."

All the people answered, "Agreed!"

Elijah then said to the prophets of Baal, "Choose one young bull and prepare it first, for there are more of you. Call upon your gods, but do not start the fire."

Taking the young bull that was turned over to them, they prepared it and called on Baal from morning to noon, saying, "Answer us, Baal!"

But there was no sound, and no one answering. And they hopped around the altar they had prepared.

When it was noon, Elijah taunted them: "Call louder, for he is a god and may be meditating, or may have retired, or may be on a journey. Perhaps he is asleep and must be awakened."

They called out louder and slashed themselves with swords and spears, as was their custom, until blood gushed over them. Noon passed and they remained in a prophetic state until the time for offering sacrifice. But there was not a sound; no one answered, and no one was listening.

Then Elijah said to all the people, "Come here to me."

When they had done so, he repaired the altar of the LORD which had been destroyed. He took twelve stones, for the number of the tribes of the sons of Jacob, to whom the LORD had said, "Your name shall be Israel."

He built an altar in honor of the LORD with the stones, and made a trench around the altar large enough for two seahs of grain. When he had arranged the wood, he cut up the young bull and laid it on the wood.

"Fill four jars with water," he said, "and pour it over the holocaust and over the wood."

"Do it again," he said, and they did it again.

"Do it a third time," he said, and they did it a third time. The water flowed around the altar, and the trench was filled with the water.

At the time for offering sacrifice, the prophet Elijah came forward and said, "LORD, God of Abraham, Isaac, and Israel, let it be known this day that you are God in Israel and that I am your servant and have done all these things by your command. Answer me, LORD! Answer me, that this people may know that you, LORD, are God and that you have brought them back to their senses."

The LORD's fire came down and consumed the holocaust, wood, stones, and dust, and it lapped up the water in the trench. Seeing this, all the people fell prostrate and said, "The LORD is God! The LORD is God!"

Then Elijah said to them, "Seize the prophets of Baal. Let none of them escape!"

They were seized, and Elijah had them brought down to the brook Kishon and there he slit their throats (1 Kgs 18:19-40).

Reflection: Elijah is a man of confidence. He knows who the real God is, and he is not scared to act nor to call upon his God and reveal God to all others.

Think about the courage it took to assemble the hundreds of prophets of Baal, the pagan god, and to face them totally alone with the crowd of Israelites sitting in the middle of the fence ready to go either way.

Think about the risk Elijah took in getting everyone assembled to agree that the god who took the sacrifice would be revealed as the real God. What if Elijah's God had decided not to act?

But what characterizes Elijah is his trust that God will not let down God's last surviving prophet. And God doesn't.

Elijah becomes a model for men who need confidence and who need to act out of a conviction that they can be vehicles for revealing who the real God is.

Opportunities, not as dramatic as Elijah's encounter on Mount Carmel, are present for doing this. When working, a man's values are often challenged by the pagan gods of others. He can demonstrate who the real God is by not participating in unjust actions, by not speaking with prejudiced lips, by not destroying the reputation of others.

At play, the real God can be revealed through honesty in playing the game. What matters is not who wins but the enthusiasm with which one plays. The opponents are not the enemy; they are fellow human beings. Respect for other people reveals the true God.

If he is married, it is in his family where a man can reveal the true God. The respect he shows to his wife and the love he lavishes on his children are windows through which they can see God. A sense of harmony, personal faith, and care for the earth further enhance and reveal God to others.

It is through Elijah that God is revealed as the Lord. It is through men and the way they present themselves and trust in God today that God can be revealed to others. The process is the same; all that is changed is the location of the action.

Meditation: How have you most recently revealed God to others? Where did this take place? What aspect of God was disclosed through you?

Prayer: God of Elijah, when your prophet was the last person who believed in you, you revealed your presence in the fire which consumed his offering. Give me the confidence and conviction of Elijah. Through me reveal yourself to others. I make this prayer in the name of Jesus Christ, your Son, who lives and reigns with you and the Holy Spirit, one God, for ever and ever. Amen.

Elisha: Receiver of the Mantle

Scripture: Elijah set out, and came upon Elisha, son of Shaphat, as he was plowing with twelve yoke of oxen; he was following the twelfth. Elijah went over to him and threw his cloak over him.

Elisha left the oxen, ran after Elijah, and said, "Please, let me kiss my father and mother goodbye, and I will follow you."

"Go back!" Elijah answered. "Have I done anything to you?"

Elisha left him and, taking the yoke of oxen, slaughtered them; he used the plowing equipment for fuel to boil their flesh, and gave it to his people to eat. Then he left and followed Elijah as his attendant.

Elijah said to Elisha, "Please stay here; the LORD has sent me on to the Jordan."

"As the LORD lives, and as you yourself live," Elisha replied, "I will not leave you."

And so the two went on together. Elijah took his mantle, rolled it up and struck the water, which divided, and both crossed over on dry ground.

When they had crossed over, Elijah said to Elisha, "Ask for whatever I may do for you, before I am taken from you."

Elisha answered, "May I receive a double portion of your spirit."

"You have asked something that is not easy," he replied. "Still, if you see me taken up from you, your wish will be granted; otherwise not."

As they walked on conversing, a flaming chariot and flaming horses came between them, and Elijah went up to heaven in a whirlwind.

When Elisha saw it happen he cried out, "My father! my father! Israel's chariots and drivers!"

But when he could no longer see him, Elisha gripped his own garment and tore it in two.

Then he picked up Elijah's mantle which had fallen from him, and went back and stood at the bank of the Jordan. Wielding the mantle which had fallen from Elijah, he struck the water in his turn and said, "Where is the LORD, the God of Elijah?"

When Elisha struck the water it divided and he crossed over (1 Kgs 19:19-21; 2 Kgs 2:6, 8-14).

Reflection: Elisha is chosen by God as Elijah's successor, as prophet in the land of Israel. He is delegated by Elijah's action of wrapping his mantle around Elisha. Then, once Elijah ascends to heaven, Elisha receives Elijah's mantle and is able to use it in the same way as did his master.

Elisha inherits Elijah's job. What shoes to fill! But he receives the same spirit which motivated Elijah and calls the people to worship the one, true God, just as his teacher had done.

Elisha is a model of one who is delegated by another to continue the work that the other began. Elisha is given responsibility by Elijah.

Today, men are often responsible for delegating responsibilities to others. Individual enterprise has been replaced with the assembly line. Everyone who works on the line is delegated to do just one small part of the whole manufacturing process. In corporate structures the president of the board or the chief executive officer must delegate a lot of responsibilities for the operation of the company to others.

Delegation occurs in religion. The Church continues to delegate men and women, who are responsible for the finances, building maintenance, liturgical and pastoral ministry, and a whole host of other jobs.

We delegate our roles to others in athletics. A team is made up of many different people, all possessing gifts. One member plays for a while and delegates another to play in his place, usually through the orchestration of a coach.

Professionals often delegate others in areas of expertise. A general medical practitioner refers a patient to a doctor who specializes in a particular area of medicine. Likewise, we call plumbers to fix the pipes in our homes and electricians to repair wiring.

Parents delegate chores to children. Husbands and wives delegate responsibilities in the family to each other.

No matter what type of delegation, the mantle is passed from one person to another. There is a job to be done, someone's shoes to be filled. The one who delegates gives the power necessary to accomplish the task.

Meditation: What have you recently delegated another to do? What has another person delegated you to do? What mantle was passed?

Prayer: God of Elisha, you chose the son of Shaphat as the successor to your prophet, Elijah, whom you swept from the earth in a whirlwind. By bestowing upon Elisha the mantle, you entrusted him with the responsibility of spreading your name among your people. Give me a share of your Spirit. Enable me to delegate responsibilities to others. When I am delegated, help me to act responsibly. I ask this in the name of the Lord Jesus Christ, your Son, who lives and reigns with you and the Holy Spirit, one God, for ever and ever. Amen.

Tobit: Man Behind the Scenes

Scripture: I, Tobit, have walked all the days of my life on the paths of truth and righteousness. I performed many charitable works for my kinsmen and my people who had been deported with me to Nineveh, in Assyria.

When I lived as a young man in my own country, Israel, the entire tribe of my forefather Naphtali had broken away from the house of David and from Jerusalem.

I, for my part, would often make the pilgrimage alone to Jerusalem for the festivals, as is prescribed for all Israel by perpetual decree. Bringing with me the first fruits of the field and the firstlings of the flock, together with a tenth of my income and the first shearing of the sheep, I would hasten to Jerusalem and present them to the priests, Aaron's sons, at the altar.

To the Levites who were doing service in Jerusalem I would give the tithe of grain, wine, olive oil, pomegranates, figs, and other fruits. And except for sabbatical years, I used to give a second tithe in money, which each year I would go and disburse in Jerusalem.

The third tithe I gave to orphans and widows, and to converts who were living with the Israelites. Every third year I would bring them this offering, and we ate it in keeping with the decree of the Mosaic law . . . .

When I reached manhood, I married Anna, a woman of our own lineage. By her I had a son whom I named Tobiah.

Now after I had been deported to Nineveh, all my brothers and relatives ate the food of heathens, but I refrained from eating that kind of food. Because of this wholehearted service of God, the Most High granted me favor and status with Shalmaneser, so that I became purchasing agent for all his needs.

During Shalmaneser's reign I performed many charitable works for my kinsmen and my people. I would give my bread to the hungry and my clothing to the naked. If I saw one of my people who had died and been thrown outside the walls of Nineveh, I would bury him. I also buried anyone whom Sennacherib slew when he returned as a fugitive from Judea during the days of judgment decreed against him by the heavenly King because of the blasphemies he had uttered.

In his rage he killed many Israelites, but I used to take their bodies by stealth and bury them; so when Sennacherib looked for them, he could not find them.

But a certain citizen of Nineveh informed the king that it was I who buried the dead. When I found out that the king knew all about me and wanted to put me to death, I went into hiding; then in my fear I took to flight. Afterward, all my property was confiscated; I was left with nothing. All that I had was taken to the king's palace, except for my wife Anna and my son Tobiah (Tob 1:3-4, 6-13, 16-20).

Reflection: Faithfulness, like that of Tobit, is a quality to be admired by men today. Faithfulness means remaining full of faith even when all else falls apart. It implies that a person trusts God when it seems that no one—and maybe not even God—is worthy of trust.

Tobit remained faithful. Even after his tribe had broken away from the confederacy which David had formed of all of the tribes of Israel, Tobit continued to make the journey to Jerusalem to offer sacrifice and to fulfill the prescribed tithes in the Temple.

After Assyria conquered the kingdom of Israel, Tobit continued to take care of his own people by risking his own death when burying the dead. Yet, because the failure to bury the dead was viewed with horror by the Jews, Tobit performed this act of charity in faithfulness to the Mosaic decrees. Indeed, Tobit is a man of truth and righteousness, faithful to God in the face of adversity.

Faithfulness is a virtue which men need to cultivate today. Just as in Tobit's time, so today remaining filled with faith is not easy. However, ample opportunities present themselves for practice of the virtue.

A man remains faithful to God and to other people when he is concerned about the needs of others. Charity may take many forms, but it must be present in a man's life. Sometimes a man may decide to make a monetary contribution to an organization which helps others. He may volunteer one day a month working in a soup kitchen or shelter. Lending his expertise to a civic service project is another way of demonstrating faithfulness to helping others.

A man remains faithful to God through weekly worship. By joining with others on Saturday evening or Sunday morning, he demonstrates that all comes from God, who is worthy of praise. Also, throughout the week, through a few moments of daily prayer in the morning or evening or while driving to work, a man can be faithful to God.

Faithfulness to others and to God demonstrates the commandment of love. If a man loves others, he also loves God and himself. Likewise, if a man loves God, he loves others and himself. Such faithfulness springs from his own inner fire and integrity. This is where a man touches the real meaning of truth and righteousness—faithfulness to himself—which blossoms as faithfulness to God.

Meditation: How are you faithful to others and to God? How are you faithful to yourself?

Prayer: God of Tobit, you made your servant walk all the days of his life on the paths of truth and righteousness in faithfulness to your law. Even when faced with the threat of death, he continued to trust that you would not abandon him. Guide my steps in faithfulness to you. Give me a deep respect for the needs of others and a willingness to praise you for your love for me. Help me to follow the Lord Jesus Christ, your Son, who lives and reigns with you and the Holy Spirit, one God, for ever and ever. Amen.

Judas Maccabeus: Revolter

Scripture: When the time came for Mathias to die, he said to his sons . . ., ". . . Judas Maccabeus, a warrior from his youth, shall be the leader of your army and direct the war against the nations. You shall also gather about you all who observe the law, and you shall avenge the wrongs of your people."

Then he blessed them, and he was united with his fathers.

Then his son Judas, who was called Maccabeus, took his place. All his brothers and all who had joined his father supported him, and they carried on Israel's war joyfully.

Then Apollonius gathered the Gentiles, together with a large army from Samaria, to fight against Israel. When Judas learned of it, he went out to meet him and defeated and killed him. Many fell wounded, and the rest fled. Their possessions were seized and the sword of Apollonius was taken by Judas, who fought with it the rest of his life.

But Seron, commander of the Syrian army, heard that Judas had gathered many about him, an assembly of faithful men ready for war.

So he said, "I will make a name for myself and win glory in the kingdom by defeating Judas and his followers, who have despised the king's command."

And again a large company of renegades advanced with him to help him take revenge on the Israelites. When he reached the ascent of Beth-horon, Judas went out to meet him with a few men.

But when they saw the army coming against them, they said to Judas: "How can we, few as we are, fight such a mighty host as this? Besides, we are weak today from fasting."

But Judas said: "It is easy for many to be overcome by a few; in the sight of Heaven there is no difference between deliverance by many or by few; for victory in war does not depend upon the size of the army, but on strength that comes from Heaven. With great presumption and lawlessness they come against us to destroy us and our wives and children and to despoil us; but we are fighting for our lives and our laws. He himself will crush them before us; so do not be afraid of them."

When he finished speaking, he rushed suddenly upon Seron and his army, who were crushed before him. Then Judas and his brothers began to be feared, and dread fell upon the Gentiles about them. His fame reached the king, and all the Gentiles talked about the battles of Judas (1 Macc 2:49, 66-67, 69; 3:1-2, 10-23, 25-26).

Reflection: After David's death, the kingdom he had established gradually began to wane, and his enemies began to wage war and lay claim to the land. Such is the state of affairs when Judas Maccabeus comes onto the scene. The Greeks have conquered the land and imposed their Gentile ways upon the Jews, forcing them into idolatry and into breaking their laws unless they were willing to die.

Judas Maccabeus represents the warrior of the just cause. While his father was a leader of the revolt against the Gentiles, Judas is known throughout history as the principal revolter. He is a man of moral and religious principles. Time after time he leads the army in revolt against Israel's enemies—and he wins.

There are times in a man's life when revolt is the only solution. All the other possibilities have been examined and none is feasible. So, a man chooses to revolt.

Sometimes the revolt may take the form of a strike. Workers walk away from their jobs in an attempt to impress their employers with the importance of benefits and wage increases. A union leader speaks for the workers with management, and through negotiations a compromise can be reached. However, without the revolt, nothing would have been gained.

Revolts take place in families. Teenagers are particularly prone to such actions. They refuse to do what their parents tell them in an attempt to gain their own identity and accept adult responsibility. If they never revolt, they may end up dependent on their parents for the rest of their lives.

A march is another form of a revolt. In the United States a march may be the most favored form of a revolt. People march for an end to racial segregation as well as for white supremacy. Anti-abortion and pro-abortion groups march on opposite sides of the street, each believing that revolt is necessary to influence a law or a decision by the Supreme Court.

Each person may engage in a personal revolt from time to time. We look at our lives and see that it is time for a change—to quit smoking, to go on a diet, to quit drinking alcohol, to do some traveling, to meet new people, to engage in spiritual growth, etc. Such a revolt is painful but necessary if we are going to adhere to any personal principles.

The guideline for any type of revolt is given by Judas Maccabeus: Many may be overcome by a few. We often think that it will take a huge army to accomplish the revolt. Judas demonstrates that it takes only a few people with God's help to accomplish what must be done. Sometimes the few give courage to the many to get involved in the revolt.

Meditation: In what type of revolt were you most recently involved? How did the few overcome the many? What revolt have you experienced in yourself? To what principles did you adhere?

Prayer: God of Judas Maccabeus, you filled your warrior with the spirit of revolt and guided him with the principles of your law. With your help he was able to purge your land of idolatry and restore the worship which you decreed. Form me in your ways. Make me a man of principle, one who is not afraid of revolt if this is the only way to accomplish your will. Hear this prayer in the name of the Lord Jesus Christ, your Son, who lives and reigns with you and the Holy Spirit, one God, for ever and ever. Amen.

Job: Patient Sufferer

Scripture: In the land of Uz there was a blameless and upright man named Job, who feared God and avoided evil. One day, when the sons of God came to present themselves before the LORD, Satan also came among them.

And the LORD said to Satan, "Whence do you come?"

Then Satan answered the LORD and said, "From roaming the earth and patrolling it."

And the LORD said to Satan, "Have you noticed my servant Job, and that there is no one on earth like him, blameless and upright, fearing God and avoiding evil?"

But Satan answered the LORD and said, "Is it for nothing that Job is God-fearing? Have you not surrounded him and his family and all that he has with your protection? You have blessed the work of his hands, and his livestock are spread over the land. But now put forth your hand and touch anything that he has, and surely he will blaspheme you to your face."

And the LORD said to Satan, "Behold, all that he has is in your power; only do not lay a hand upon his person."

So Satan went forth from the presence of the LORD.

And so one day, while his sons and his daughters were eating and drinking wine in the house of their eldest brother, a messenger came to Job and said, "The oxen were plowing and the asses grazing beside them, and the Sabeans carried them off in a raid. They put the herdsmen to the sword, and I alone have escaped to tell you."

While he was yet speaking, another came and said, "Lightning has fallen from heaven and struck the sheep and their shepherds and consumed them; and I alone have escaped to tell you."

While he was yet speaking, another came and said, "The Chaldeans formed three columns, seized the camels, carried them off, and put those tending them to the sword, and I alone have escaped to tell you."

While he was yet speaking, another came and said, "Your sons and daughters were eating and drinking wine in the house of their eldest brother, when suddenly a great wind came across the desert and smote the four corners of the house. It fell upon the young people and they are dead; and I alone have escaped to tell you."

Then Job began to tear his cloak and cut off his hair. He cast himself prostrate upon the ground, and said,

> "Naked I came forth from my mother's womb,
> and naked shall I go back again.
> The LORD gave and the LORD has taken away;
> blessed be the name of the LORD!"

In all of this Job did not sin, nor did he say anything disrespectful of God (Job 1:1, 6-22).

Reflection: Job emerges from the pages of the Bible as the model of a man who suffers gracefully. Or to put it another way, Job understands "tough suffering."

Job does not blame anyone for his suffering. He understands that suffering is a part of living. Most of the great lessons of life are learned through suffering. The best teacher is suffering.

There is no answer to why we suffer, other than to say that it is an integral part of life. Anyone who truly wishes to experience life must also be ready and willing to suffer.

In the midst of his suffering, Job recognizes that what he had owned was only entrusted to him for a time. He emerged from his mother's womb with nothing, and he will one day die with nothing. While possessions are useful on this side of the grave, they are useless on the other side of it.

All things are given to us by God, as Job so clearly understands. We are only stewards for the duration of our pilgrimage on earth. Try as hard as we might, we can never really lay claim to anything. When we die, our deed of ownership is meaningless.

Men suffer. Some suffer silently through the breaking of relationships—marriage and friendship. Suddenly receiving a pink slip at work brings forth a certain amount of suffering. Disagreements with a spouse is suffering. Trying to decide between two good choices fosters suffering. Broken bones and disease bring suffering into a man's life.

We try to prevent it. We try to pretend that it is not there. But suffering is as real as diamond etched on glass. Suffering is woven throughout the fabric of our lives. It shapes us and forms us, just as it molded Job into the type of person he was.

In the midst of suffering—which has no reason and to which there are no answers—all we can do is to praise God for what we have and are. Suffering is a gift, a gracious gift, entrusted to us by God.

Meditation: What was the last suffering you endured? Did you blame anyone for it? Did you try to reason why you had to suffer? How did your suffering make you a better person? What gift did God give to you?

Prayer: God of Job, you made your servant blameless and upright, a man who feared you and avoided evil. Even when untold suffering came his way, Job did not turn away from you but rather realized that nothing was his to begin with. Give me patience in my suffering. Enable me to bless your name with that of your Son, the Lord Jesus Christ, and the Holy Spirit, who lives and reigns with you, one God, for ever and ever. Amen.

Isaiah: Scared of God

Scripture: . . . I saw the Lord seated on a high and lofty throne, with the train of his garment filling the temple. Seraphim were stationed above; each of them had six wings: with two they veiled their faces, with two they veiled their feet, and with two they hovered aloft.

"Holy, holy, holy is the LORD of hosts!" they cried one to the other. "All the earth is filled with his glory!"

At the sound of that cry, the frame of the door shook and the house was filled with smoke.

Then I said, "Woe is me, I am doomed! For I am a man of unclean lips, living among a people of unclean lips; yet my eyes have seen the King, the LORD of hosts!"

Then one of the seraphim flew to me, holding an ember which he had taken with tongs from the altar. He touched my mouth with it.

"See," he said, "now that this has touched your lips, your wickedness is removed, your sin purged."

Then I heard the voice of the Lord saying, "Whom shall I send? Who will go for us?"

"Here I am;" I said; "send me!" (Isa 6:1-8)

Reflection: Fear is not an emotion which most men will admit having. Fear indicates vulnerability, and most men prefer an image of themselves as fearless. They go courageously into battle. They defend their families. They design and build huge machines and repair them when they break down.

Isaiah represents the man who is not afraid of fear. Once he has a vision of God, he presumes that he will die, since no one had ever seen God and lived to tell about it. But the awesome experience does not leave Isaiah dead. In fact, he is purified by God's fiery grace and made acceptable by God before God.

It is out of his fear that Isaiah finds his strength to answer God's question, "Whom shall I send?" Like a student wanting to be called on by the teacher by waving his hand, Isaiah declares, "Send me." It would be incorrect to say that Isaiah was fearless; it is out of his fear that he touches God's grace within himself and is able to accept his mission.

Isaiah becomes a mode of how men can look at fear. Instead of pretending that they are not scared, men can reach down into themselves, touch their fear, and permit its graced existence to buoy them up in a time of crisis.

When a man must confront another person about a problem which the other is causing at work, he is usually scared of making an enemy of that other person. Sometimes, after thinking about the psychological energy it will take for the confrontation, a man may decide to just drop the issue and hope that it will go away. But if he can acknowledge his fear, he might be able to find the strength he needs within it to confront the other and deal successfully with the problem.

A man who is part of a family may be fearful when it comes to helping the family make a decision, such as a change in career, a move to another town, or a change in schools for children. He may ask himself, "How can I make the right decision?" By touching the fear within and accepting its grace, he may not always make the right decision, but he will make a good one.

What Isaiah declares is that fear does not debilitate us. On the contrary, fear is another experience of God at work in our lives. It can empower a person to act, like it gave Isaiah courage to accept the mission which God presented to him.

Meditation: When were you recently afraid? Of what were you fearful? How did you deal with your fear? Did you admit its existence and find strength from it or fear it?

Prayer: God of Isaiah, with fire you made your servant acceptable in your presence. As he acknowledged his fear, Isaiah also experienced your grace and was able to accept the mission you gave to him. Help me to find strength in my fears. Enable me to recognize your grace at work in my life. Hear this prayer through the Lord Jesus Christ, your Son, who lives and reigns with you and the Holy Spirit, one God, for ever and ever. Amen.

Jeremiah: Stubborn Is Good

Scripture: The word of the Lord came to me thus:

> Before I formed you in the womb I knew you,
> before you were born I dedicated you,
> a prophet to the nations I appointed you.
> "Ah, Lord God!" I said,
> "I know not how to speak; I am too young."
> But the Lord answered me,
> Say not, "I am too young."
> To whomever I send you, you shall go;
> whatever I command you, you shall speak.
> Have no fear before them,
> because I am with you to deliver you, says the Lord.

Then the Lord extended his hand and touched my mouth, saying,

> See, I place my words in your mouth!
> This day I set you
> over nations and over kingdoms,
> To root up and to tear down,
> to destroy and to demolish,
> to build and to plant (Jer 1:4-10).

Reflection: Jeremiah is the example of a prophet who is stubborn and reluctant to do what God requests. But God uses his stubbornness to accomplish what God wants. The humanness of Jeremiah shines through when he falls into despair and declares that God has duped him. Jeremiah even curses the day that he was born and calls God every derogatory name that he can remember.

God, however, is bigger than Jeremiah. God can take Jeremiah's outbursts. God tells him to repent and that God will take him back and renew his mission to the people. Reluctantly Jeremiah agrees.

Many men are noted for their stubbornness. Stubbornness is that inability to be open to a variety of possibilities; it is seeing the world through one lens and not being able to admit that other lenses exist. A stubborn man says that there is one correct way of doing something and that is his way.

Stubbornness can cause more problems than it solves. Not being able to be flexible can leave a man all alone with his own opinion. Holding out can isolate a man.

Stubborn child-rearing techniques can cause division in familial structures. Stubborn practices at work can destroy a business. Sometimes a man's stubbornness can lead to consequences which are fatal.

On the other hand, stubbornness can be good when viewed from the perspective of courageously upholding principles. God chose Jeremiah and used his stubbornness to call Israel to repentance and to a change of heart. When Jeremiah rebelled, God called him out of his stubbornness to repent, and the prophet responded over and over again to God's initiation.

Managing a drive through the stubbornness that isolates and that which enables men to hold fast to principles is not an easy task. However, it is one which Jeremiah embraced and one in which God was discovered to be at work.

Meditation: When have you been stubborn in the sense of just not wanting to see another way? When have you been stubborn in the sense of upholding principles which you believe in?

Prayer: God of Jeremiah, you made your prophet stubborn in your ways so that he could call nations and kingdoms to repentance. Even when he became disillusioned, you placed a fire in his heart and he grew weary until he preached your word. Guide my stubbornness in your ways and do not permit me to isolate myself from the new life to which you have called me through your Son, the Lord Jesus Christ, who lives and reigns with you and the Holy Spirit, one God, for ever and ever. Amen.

Ezekiel: Hungry for the Word

Scripture: . . . I fell upon my face and heard a voice that said to me: Son of man, stand up! I wish to speak with you. As he spoke to me, spirit entered into me and set me on my feet, and I heard the one who was speaking say to me:

Son of man, I am sending you to the Israelites, rebels who have rebelled against me; they and their fathers have revolted against me to this very day. Hard of face and obstinate of heart are they to whom I am sending you. But you shall say to them:

Thus says the LORD God! And whether they heed or resist—for they are a rebellious house—they shall know that a prophet has been among them. But as for you, son of man, fear neither them nor their words when they contradict you and reject you. . . . Neither fear their words nor be dismayed at their looks, for they are a rebellious house.

As for you, son of man, obey me when I speak to you: be not rebellious like this house of rebellion, but open your mouth and eat what I shall give you.

It was then I saw a hand stretched out to me, in which was a written scroll which he unrolled before me. It was covered with writing front and back, and written on it was: Lamentation and wailing and woe!

He said to me: Son of man, eat what is before you; eat this scroll, then go speak to the house of Israel. So I opened my mouth and he gave me the scroll to eat. Son of man, he then said to me, feed your belly and fill your stomach with this scroll I am giving you. I ate it, and it was as sweet as honey in my mouth. He said: Son of man, go now to the house of Israel, and speak my words to them.

Not to a people with difficult speech and barbarous language am I sending you, nor to the many peoples . . . whose words you cannot understand. If I were to send you to these, they would listen to you; but the house of Israel will refuse to listen to you, since they will not listen to me. For the whole house of Israel is stubborn of brow and obstinate in heart. But I will make your face as hard as theirs and your brow as stubborn as theirs, like diamond, harder than flint. Fear them not, nor be dismayed at their looks, for they are a rebellious house (Ezek 2:1-6, 8-9; 3:1-9).

Reflection: How does a man present, instruct, or teach anyone anything? The answer is that he must first learn it himself. Therefore, if a man is going to present the results of a study which he conducted, he has to have first analyzed the results. Likewise, if a man is going to instruct people in a new technique, he must have mastered the technique himself. A teacher knows that the best way to be a good teacher is to know his or her material as best as possible.

What this implies is that a man must first digest that which he will give. He must make it a part of himself by getting it within. Then, he speaks or presents or instructs or teaches out of the feast of knowledge upon which he has gorged himself.

God gives the prophet Ezekiel a scroll, which he eats. The scroll represents the word which God wants announced to the rebellious house of Israel. The only way for Ezekiel to preach God's word is to master it first. He has to get it inside of himself. So, he eats the scroll with the word of God written upon it. Then, he is sent to Israel to deliver God's message.

Like the people Ezekiel encountered, those to whom we are sent with a presentation or an instruction or a class often are not receptive. Sometimes they are simply rebellious. This is because anytime anyone presents something new a rebellion is likely. People do not like change; we prefer to continue doing what we do the way we know how to do it.

But to remain in such a state contradicts the God who calls people to conversion, to a constant process of a change of heart. Throughout the Bible God seems to be portrayed as a God of change. God is always calling people to see things the way that God sees them, to walk in God's paths, to hear God's word.

When a man is sent with a message of change or a new technique or a new instruction, he must be like Ezekiel—fully gorged on what he is going to present and confident that it is through him that God calls people to a change of heart.

Meditation: When have you eaten a lot of information before making a presentation of any kind? How have you eaten the word of God and been changed? What is the greatest obstacle to change?

Prayer: God of Ezekiel, you entrusted your word to the son of man, who, after eating it, spoke it to your rebellious people, Israel. Give me a greater understanding of your word that I might feast upon it and it might effect a change in my life. Keep me faithful to the process of a change of heart that I might faithfully follow your Son, the Lord Jesus Christ, who lives and reigns with you and the Holy Spirit, one God, for ever and ever. Amen.

Daniel: Keeper of the Lion's Den

Scripture: Darius decided to appoint over his entire kingdom one hundred and twenty satraps, to safeguard his interests; these were accountable to three supervisors, one of whom was Daniel.

Daniel outshone all the supervisors and satraps because an extraordinary spirit was in him, and the king thought of giving him authority over the entire kingdom. Therefore the supervisors and satraps tried to find grounds for accusation against Daniel as regards the administration. But they could accuse him of no wrongdoing; because he was trustworthy, no fault of neglect or misconduct was to be found in him.

Then these men said to themselves, "We shall find no grounds for accusation against this Daniel unless by way of the law of his God."

So these supervisors and satraps went thronging to the king and said to him, "King Darius, live forever! All the supervisors of the kingdom, the prefects, satraps, nobles, and governors are agreed that the following prohibition ought to be put in force by royal decree: no one is to address any petition to god or man for thirty days, except to you, O king; otherwise he shall be cast into a den of lions. Now, O king, issue the prohibition over your signature, immutable and irrevocable under Mede and Persian law."

So King Darius signed the prohibition and made it law.

Even after Daniel heard that his law had been signed, he continued his custom of going home to kneel in prayer and give thanks to his God in the upper chamber three times a day, with the windows open toward Jerusalem. So these men rushed in and found Daniel praying and pleading before his God.

Then they went to remind the king about the prohibition: "Did you not decree, O king, that no one is to address a petition to god or man for thirty days except to you, O king; otherwise, he shall be cast into a den of lions?"

The king answered them, "The decree is absolute, irrevocable under the Mede and Persian law."

To this they replied, "Daniel, the Jewish exile, has paid no attention to you, O king, or to the decree you issued; three times a day he offers his prayer."

The king was deeply grieved at this news and he made up his mind to save Daniel; he worked till sunset to rescue him. But these men insisted.

"Keep in mind, O king," they said, "that under the Mede and Persian law every royal prohibition or decree is irrevocable."

So the king ordered Daniel to be brought and cast into the lions' den.

To Daniel he said, "May your God, whom you serve so constantly, save you."

To forestall any tampering, the king sealed with his own ring and the rings of the lords the stone that had been brought to block the opening of the den.

Then the king returned to his palace for the night; he refused to eat and he dismissed the entertainers. Since sleep was impossible for him, the king rose very early the next morning and hastened to the lions' den.

As he drew near, he cried out to Daniel sorrowfully, "O Daniel, servant of the living God, has the God whom you serve so constantly been able to save you from the lions?"

Daniel answered the king: "O king, live forever! My God has sent his angel and closed the lions' mouths so that they have not hurt me. For I have been found innocent before him; neither to you have I done any harm, O king!"

This gave the king great joy. At this order Daniel was removed from the den, unhurt because he trusted in his God. The king then ordered the men who had accused Daniel, along with their children and their wives, to be cast into the lions' den. Before they reached the bottom of the den, the lions overpowered them and crushed all their bones (Dan 6:2-25).

Reflection: After reading the selection above from the Book of Daniel, a man might ask for clarification as to which lions was Daniel thrown. It seems like all the supervisors of the kingdom are the real lions, who set up the trap into which Daniel falls.

But Daniel is really the keeper of the lions' den. What the supervisors see is not what God sees. And because they do not see the way God sees, they are doomed before they begin. Their plot to destroy Daniel is likewise a plot to destroy the king, who recognizes that he has been used and must get rid of those who would make him look foolish by the death of the man to whom he was ready to entrust his kingdom.

Because of Daniel's trust in God, he was delivered. Because of Daniel's trust in God, the king was converted. Because of Daniel's trust in God, God was praised and shown to be the only true God.

The supervisors of the kingdom presumed power, when they really had none; they were only the supervisors and not the king. Daniel presumed powerlessness, because that was the situation in which he found himself. Daniel knew that God specializes in reversals. And so it happened: The lions only devoured those who first attempted to devour others!

Daniel stands as model of a man who knows how to keep lions. First, a man must know his place. He is not God, but he may have a level of responsibility in his family, at work, during play. Second, realizing his place in the world, he knows that there are always others who are more powerful. Maneuvering through the maze helps one to recognize how powerless one really is.

When a man is placed in such a crossfire as was Daniel, he often responds by fighting back. Daniel, as keeper of the lions, reminds us to trust in God. God saves those who are just and true. Through salvation God enables others to believe.

A man's greatest temptation is to save himself through his own power and strength. To do so, however, puts him in the position of the supervisors of the kingdom—seeking more power. God is not interested in power; God is interested in how well a man can trust God to take care of things in God's way and in God's own time.

Meditation: What experiences have you had of being a keeper of lions? How did God save you? How did you place your trust in God?

Prayer: God of Daniel, when your servant was placed in the lions' den, you saved him from the power of those who sought his life and made him greater than he was before. Through him you enabled others to recognize you as the one true God of all nations. Strengthen my faith and trust. Keep me from getting entangled in the nets of power. Help me to follow in the steps of Jesus Christ, your Son, who lives and reigns with you and the Holy Spirit, one God, for ever and ever. Amen.

Hosea: Remarriage

Scripture: The word of the Lord that came to Hosea. . . . In the beginning of the Lord's speaking to Hosea, the Lord said to Hosea:

> Go, take a harlot wife and harlot's children,
> for the land gives itself to harlotry,
> turning away from the Lord.

So he went and took Gomer . . ., and she conceived and bore him a son. Then the Lord said to him:

> Give him the name Jezreel,
> for in a little while
> I will punish the house of Jehu
> for the bloodshed of Jezreel
> And bring to an end the kingdom
> of the house of Israel;
> On that day I will break the bow of Israel
> in the valley of Jezreel.

When she conceived again and bore a daughter, the Lord said to him:

> Give her the name Lo-ruhama;
> I no longer feel pity for the house of Israel:
> rather, I abhor them utterly.
> Yet for the house of Judah I feel pity;
> I will save them by the Lord, their God;
> But I will not save them by war,
> by sword or bow, by horses or horsemen.

After she weaned Lo-ruhama, she conceived and bore a son. Then the LORD said:

> Give him the name Lo-ammi,
> for you are not my people,
> and I will not be your God.
> Protest against your mother, protest!
> for she is not my wife,
> and I am not her husband.
> Let her remove her harlotry from before her,
> her adultery from between her breasts,
> Or I will strip her naked,
> leaving her as on the day of her birth;
> I will make her like the desert,
> reduce her to an arid land,
> and slay her with thirst.
> I will have no pity on her children,
> for they are the children of harlotry.
> Yes, their mother has played the harlot;
> she that conceived them has acted shamefully (Hos 1:1-8; 2:4-7).

Reflection: What kind of a man marries a prostitute? What kind of a man is wed to a harlot, a woman of the night, a lady of the streets, a whore? These are harsh, negative words, but they are not nearly as harsh and negative as the words of God spoken through the prophet Hosea, who takes a harlot for his wife.

A man, like Hosea, who marries a prostitute, must be very confident and loving and trusting. He must be able to let go of his wife's former occupation. Such a man must be willing to not look back, but move on with the future.

Hosea's taking of a harlot wife represents Israel. Collectively, God refers to his people as a whore, because they divorced themselves from God and God's ways and began to worship foreign gods. Idolatry is biblical harlotry. God was husband to his people, God's wife, but they took up the occupation of a prostitute, worshiping other gods.

Today, the taking of a harlot wife is still a possibility, but in language which is less harsh, it might be referred to as remarriage. A lot of men marry a woman who has been previously married and who may have children from the former marriage. Immediately, men assume not only the role of husband but that of father—to some degree, depending upon the ages of the children.

A man's new role can be filled with problems. His choice of a wife can damage his reputation. She can become the rumor of the town. People who are familiar with both of them can choose to not invite or include them in social functions. Children born from the union may suffer discrimination in school.

Hosea's marriage to a harlot, however, is used to demonstrate that when people are unfaithful to God, God is always faithful. God takes back his people; God remarries them when they return to God's offer of the marriage covenant. Hosea took a prostitute as a wife, just like God took his people as his wife time and time again.

And in a similar way, men are not to despise women who have engaged in harlotry but to respect them for the human beings they are. If God can forgive a whole people who prostituted itself, then we can forgive those who have acted in a similar manner.

Meditation: Are you or do you know someone who is remarried? How are you/is he adapting to it? What problems do you/has he encountered? How are you/is he like Hosea?

Prayer: God of Hosea, in order to demonstrate your willingness to assume your role as husband to your people Israel, you called your prophet to take a harlot for his wife. Give me the courage to forgive. Give me the ability to respect every person. Hear my prayer through the Lord Jesus Christ, your Son, who lives and reigns with you and the Holy Spirit, one God, for ever and ever. Amen.

Jonah: From the Fish's Perspective

Scripture: This is the word of the LORD that came to Jonah . . .: "Set out for the great city of Nineveh, and preach against it; their wickedness has come up before me."

But Jonah made ready to flee to Tarshish away from the LORD. He went down to Joppa, found a ship going to Tarshish, paid the fare, and went aboard to journey with them to Tarshish, away from the LORD.

The LORD, however, hurled a violent wind upon the sea, and in the furious tempest that arose the ship was on the point of breaking up. Then the mariners became frightened and each one cried to his god. To lighten the ship for themselves, they threw its cargo into the sea.

Meanwhile, Jonah had gone down into the hold of the ship, and lay there fast asleep.

The captain came to him and said, "What are you doing asleep? Rise up, call upon your God! Perhaps God will be mindful of us so that we may not perish."

Then they said to one another, "Come, let us cast lots to find out on whose account we have met with this misfortune."

So they cast lots, and thus singled out Jonah.

"Tell us," they said, "what is your business? Where do you come from? What is your country, and to what people do you belong?"

"I am a Hebrew," Jonah answered them; "I worship the LORD, the God of heaven, who made the sea and the dry land."

Now the men were seized with great fear and said to him, "How could you do such a thing!"—They knew that he was fleeing from the LORD, because he had told them.—"What shall we do with you," they asked, "that the sea may quiet down for us?"

For the sea was growing more and more turbulent.

Jonah said to them, "Pick me up and throw me into the sea, that it may quiet down for you; since I know it is because of me that this violent storm has come upon you."

Still the men rowed hard to regain the land, but they could not, for the sea grew ever more turbulent. Then they cried to the Lord: "We beseech you, O Lord, let us not perish for taking this man's life; do not charge us with shedding innocent blood, for you, Lord, have done as you saw fit."

Then they took Jonah and threw him into the sea, and the sea's raging abated. Struck with great fear of the Lord, the men offered sacrifice and made vows to him.

But the Lord sent a large fish, that swallowed Jonah; and he remained in the belly of the fish three days and three nights. Then the Lord commanded the fish to spew Jonah upon the shore.

The word of the Lord came to Jonah a second time: "Set out for the great city of Nineveh, and announce to it the message that I will tell you."

So Jonah made ready and went to Nineveh, according to the Lord's bidding.

Now Nineveh was an enormously large city; it took three days to go through it. Jonah began his journey through the city, and had gone but a single day's walk announcing, "Forty days more and Nineveh shall be destroyed," when the people of Nineveh believed God; they proclaimed a fast and all of them, great and small, put on sackcloth.

When the news reached the king of Nineveh, he rose from his throne, laid aside his robe, covered himself with sackcloth, and sat in the ashes.

Then he had this proclaimed throughout Nineveh, by decree of the king and his nobles: "Neither man nor beast, neither cattle nor sheep, shall taste anything; they shall not eat, nor shall they drink water. Man and beast shall be covered with sackcloth and call loudly to God; every man shall turn from his evil way and from the violence he has in hand. Who knows, God may relent and forgive, and withhold his blazing wrath, so that we shall not perish."

When God saw by their actions how they turned from their evil way, he repented of the evil that he had threatened to do to them; he did not carry it out (Jonah 1:1-16; 2:1, 11; 3:1-10).

Reflection: How many times does a man have to hear God's call before he listens and acts upon it? The answer to the question differs from man to man. However, it is safe to say that most men are like Jonah; they do not respond immediately and may run away.

In other words, men often engage in combat or a war of wills with God. A man hears God's call to marriage, but he runs away from it, saying that he is not ready to settle down and to raise a family. Every time he tries to run he is stopped by the woman who wants to marry him, by a job that will not let him transfer, by a school which will not accept his academic credits. After the second or third attempt, he listens and responds.

A man may first hear God's call to some form of religious life in his younger years, but he decides that he must test it. So, he goes to college and engages in all types of anti-religious behavior. He stops attending church regularly. He begins to speak negatively about organized religion. After acquiring a career and becoming successful, however, he cannot take God's call any more and so he decides to respond.

God issues calls to men to act ethically, to treat other people with basic human dignity, to eliminate prejudice, to help the poor, etc. In most cases men run away only later to respond to God's call.

Maybe men just need time in the belly of the fish. From the perspective of the fish, the belly is an isolated, quiet place. It is conducive to reflection. In a way it is like a womb, in which new life is nourished and from which it emerges.

When Jonah is spewed upon the beach of Nineveh, he is born again. This time when God speaks, Jonah responds, and God makes Jonah's preaching effective for all the people of Nineveh, from the king to the peasant—and even the animals!

Jonah is a model not only of the man who runs away from God, but the man whom God finds and to whom God gives new life. From the view of the fish, Jonah is a bite of food which cannot be digested, cargo that was tossed overboard. To Nineveh, Jonah was a source of new life.

Meditation: When have you run away from God? How long did you spend in the belly of the fish? What task did you ultimately accept from God? How did God make you successful?

Prayer: God of Jonah, when your prophet ran away from you, you gave him new birth and made him responsive to your word. Jonah's preaching was effective and you demonstrated that you are the God of all nations with mercy for all peoples. Help me to recognize your call and give me the grace to respond to your will. While I am in the belly of the fish, enlighten my mind and heart through the Lord Jesus Christ, your Son, who lives and reigns with you and the Holy Spirit, one God, for ever and ever. Amen.

John the Baptist: Preacher in the Desert

Scripture: In those days John the Baptist appeared, preaching in the desert of Judea [and] saying, "Repent, for the kingdom of heaven is at hand!"

It was of him that the prophet Isaiah had spoken when he said:
"A voice of one crying out in the desert,
'Prepare the way of the Lord,
make straight his paths.'"

John wore clothing made of camel's hair and had a leather belt around his waist. His food was locusts and wild honey.

At that time Jerusalem, all Judea, and the whole region around the Jordan were going out to him and were being baptized by him in the Jordan River as they acknowledged their sins.

When he saw many of the Pharisees and Sadducees coming to his baptism, he said to them, "You brood of vipers! Who warned you to flee from the coming wrath? Produce good fruit as evidence of your repentance. And do not presume to say to yourselves, 'We have Abraham as our father.' For I tell you, God can raise up children to Abraham from these stones. Even now the ax lies at the root of the trees. Therefore every tree that does not bear good fruit will be cut down and thrown into the fire. I am baptizing you with water, for repentance, but the one who is coming after me is mightier than I. I am not worthy to carry his sandals. He will baptize you with the holy Spirit and fire. His winnowing fan is in his hand. He will clear his threshing floor and gather his wheat into his barn, but the chaff he will burn with unquenchable fire" (Matthew 3:1-12).

Reflection: John the Baptist stands on the desert bank of the Jordan River and gives the impression that he is a mad man. He screams about repentance. He intimidates whoever comes closer to him. He refers to the leaders of the people as snakes. Dressed in a camel's hair wrap around, gathered at his waist with a leather belt, some of the honey can still be seen caught in his beard along with particles of the bugs he has been eating.

John the Baptist not only preaches in the desert, he preaches from the desert—one which exists within himself. It is out of his emptiness, desertedness, that John is able to prepare the way for one who is mightier than he and who will set the world on fire. In comparison, John is merely a match to the raging forest fire that Jesus will set upon the earth.

John represents the wild dimension of men. As so often happens, men can become tamed; they are no longer on fire with anything. Their enthusiasm has been doused. Life becomes a series of ever-repeated boring experiences. They need John's wild fire enthusiasm.

Such fire comes from spending time in the desert. It is in the desert where the sun burns the brightest. In the desert a man can be purified of all distractions, boredoms, and petty concerns. Is it any wonder that so many people are attracted to backpacking, hiking, and camping out in the desert?

After spending time in the desert, a man becomes a desert. His wildness comes through; his enthusiasm is refreshed; his fire is rekindled. Like John the Baptist he begins to recognize the one who is greater than he is and he confronts all that is not true. A man's personal desert enables him to see all that is fake and deceptive and to recognize all the masks which people wear.

There is an urgency which results from the desert experience—both the physical and the spiritual. The time is now. It is like an ax chopping down a tree; only a few more strokes and the timber will fall. It is like the old method of separating chaff from wheat by tossing them into the air and watching the wind blow away the chaff while the wheat falls below to the floor.

Such a reawakened wildness in men is part of what makes them men. With an enthusiasm, like fire in their bellies, they go out to set the world on fire.

Meditation: When have you felt that you were on fire? What type of desert experience(s) preceded your fiery enthusiasm? Where is your favorite desert? How does God speak to you there?

Prayer: God of John the Baptist, you prepared the last of your prophets by sending him to the desert where you could warm his heart with your love. Like a blazing fire he emerged to preach repentance and to prepare the way for the coming of your Son, Jesus Christ. Set me on fire with the gift of your Holy Spirit. Give me the enthusiasm and urgency of Jesus, who lives and reigns with you and the Holy Spirit, one God, for ever and ever. Amen.

Peter: Flexible and Passionate

Scripture: When [Jesus and his disciples] had finished breakfast, Jesus said to Simon Peter, "Simon, son of John, do you love me more than these?"

He said to him, "Yes, Lord, you know that I love you."

He said to him, "Feed my lambs."

He then said to him a second time, "Simon, son of John, do you love me?"

He said to him, "Yes, Lord, you know that I love you."

He said to him, "Tend my sheep."

He said to him the third time, "Simon, son of John, do you love me?"

Peter was distressed that he had said to him a third time, "Do you love me?" and he said to him, "Lord, you know everything; you know that I love you."

[Jesus] said to him, "Feed my sheep."

"Amen, amen, I say to you, when you were younger, you used to dress yourself and go where you wanted; but when you grow old, you will stretch out your hands, and someone else will dress you and lead you where you do not want to go."

He said this signifying by what kind of death he would glorify God.

And when he had said this, he said to him, "Follow me" (John 21:15-19).

Reflection: Peter is a character who has fascinated men for hundreds of years because he combines both flexibility and passion into one personality. He is flexible insofar as he knows how to get out of a sticky situation. He is passionate as he both solemnly denies his master and professes his love for him.

Peter is a dramatic model. When the going gets tough, he disappears from the picture. Peter is faced with being accused of being Jesus' accomplice, but he denies it. A three-fold denial, it seems, comes easy to Peter.

It is no wonder then that the added chapter to John's Gospel contains a three-fold passionate profession of love. With the same abandon of denial, Peter declares his love for Jesus, and he is restored with a mission of tending the lambs and sheep of Jesus' flock. Who better to be entrusted with hard-to-manage, usually stupid and wandering lambs and sheep than Peter?

Jesus' final words in this section is worthy of our attention. He says to Peter, "Follow me." Why? Because men are always being called back to follow the master. They stray away in flexible denial, but they are called back to passionate love. It was these two sides of Peter that interested Jesus; it is these two sides of men today that still interest Jesus.

In a moment of flexible denial, a man tells his wife a lie—that he was not out drinking or with another woman or whatever. Of course, she intuitively knows the truth. When he admits the truth and is forgiven, his denial turns into passionate love.

A little cheating on income taxes or some other unethical practices demonstrate a man's flexible denial. However, his love for his country and his own integrity often move him to make amends in some passionate way.

Bishops, priests, and deacons in the Church often find themselves flexibly denying what they know is the truth in order to avoid conflicts and to try to keep everyone happy. Sooner or later they hear those words, "Follow me," and passionate love re-enters their lives. The gospel is preached as it is written.

All men can look to Peter as a model. He represents both sides of the coin. That is what attracted him to Jesus. Such a type of character is what attracts men to Jesus today.

Meditation: When have you most recently experienced yourself flexibly denying and then passionately loving? Who said to you, "Follow me"?

Prayer: God of Peter, your Son, the Lord Jesus Christ, not only forgave Simon's denial but entrusted to him the care of his lambs and sheep. In my moments of denial help me to hear his words of "Follow me" that I might acknowledge again my love of him who lives and reigns with you and the Holy Spirit, one God, for ever and ever. Amen.

Paul: Man's Intellectual

Scripture: Paul, a slave of Christ Jesus, called to be an apostle and set apart for the gospel of God, which he promised previously through his prophets in the holy scriptures, the gospel about his Son, descended from David according to the flesh, but established as Son of God in power according to the spirit of holiness through resurrection from the dead, Jesus Christ our Lord.

Through him we have received the grace of apostleship, to bring about the obedience of faith, for the sake of his name, among all the Gentiles, among whom are you also, who are called to belong to Jesus Christ; to all the beloved of God in Rome, called to be holy. Grace to you and peace from God our Father and the Lord Jesus Christ (Rom 1:1-7).

Reflection: Paul writes with the flare of a man who is not only educated but stands back and reflects on his own experiences. He refers to himself as a slave, one who is owned by another—Christ. And yet in the same sentence he acknowledges that he is also an apostle, one who is sent with the gospel, the good news of God, to all people to awaken them to faith and the free obedience which it entails.

Paul's intellectuality and theologizing is a model for professional men, such as lawyers, doctors, theologians, professors, etc. These types of men are educated, meaning that they have spent many hours in the classroom learning theories and applying them.

What Paul represents is the ability to use one's intellectual abilities as a filter to reflect on experiences and to make sense out of them. This is not meant to imply that men who are not as educated as professionals cannot engage in the same process, but we usually predicate this process of professionals and look to them for their insights.

What is the process? It begins with knowledge of a variety of perspectives—ways of viewing, theories. The more theories a man knows the better able he is to analyze his experiences. The second step involves awareness of reality. So often reality is perceived only through sight instead of using all the other senses.

The third part is asking, "What does this experience mean?" This question is not meant to be given only one answer. By examining the experience through the various lenses of learning and perspectives, a man assigns a number of meanings to his experience.

Then, he tests each of them to see which is the best or which best explains what he has experienced. The testing is done through further analytical reflection and/or dialogue with others.

The last step is sharing the insight with others. This can take the form of sharing a reflection, writing a book or an article, or preaching a homily.

This is what Paul did. He was trained in the best of intellectual schools. But he experienced a different reality when he encountered Jesus the Christ, who caused him to ask new questions about salvation. After reflecting and testing his ideas, he discovered that a new world order had been established. He shared his ideas and insights with us through his letters.

Thus, he stands as a model for professional men today of not only how to do the process, but as a representative of one who engaged in the process frequently.

Meditation: Choose a past experience of your life and, using the process explained above, reflect upon it and search out its meanings. What have you learned?

Prayer: God of Paul, you called Saul to be a slave and apostle of your Son, Jesus Christ. By reflecting on his experiences, you filled him with new understanding so that he was able to proclaim to the nations the good news of your love. With your Holy Spirit as a guide, help me to reflect on the experiences of my life and enable me to share them with your people through Jesus Christ, your Son, who lives and reigns with you and the Holy Spirit, one God, for ever and ever. Amen.

Jesus Christ: Tragic Hero

Scripture: [The soldiers] brought [Jesus] to the place of Golgotha (which is translated Place of the Skull). They gave him wine drugged with myrrh, but he did not take it. Then they crucified him and divided his garments by casting lots for them to see what each should take.

It was nine o'clock in the morning when they crucified him.

The inscription of the charge against him read, "The King of the Jews." With him they crucified two revolutionaries, one on his right and one on his left.

Those passing by reviled him, shaking their heads and saying, "Aha! You who would destroy the temple and rebuild it in three days, save yourself by coming down from the cross."

Likewise the chief priests, with the scribes, mocked him among themselves and said, "He saved others; he cannot save himself. Let the Messiah, the King of Israel, come down now from the cross that we may see and believe."

Those who were crucified with him also kept abusing him.

At noon darkness came over the whole land until three in the afternoon. And at three o'clock Jesus cried out in a loud voice, "Eloi, Eloi, lema sabachthani?" which is translated, "My God, my God, why have you forsaken me?"

Some of the bystanders who heard it said, "Look, he is calling Elijah."

One of them ran, soaked a sponge with wine, put it on a reed, and gave it to him to drink, saying, "Wait, let us see if Elijah comes to take him down."

Jesus gave a loud cry and breathed his last.

The veil of the sanctuary was torn in two from top to bottom.

When the centurion who stood facing him saw how he breathed his last he said, "Truly this man was the Son of God!" (Mark 15:22-39)

Reflection: One aspect of life with which men have the most difficulty dealing is that of tragedy—their own or other's. Tragedy, an event which leaves one feeling helpless and paralyzed, can be accompanied by the thought that God has abandoned the person. A man feels all alone when confronting a tragic situation.

Jesus Christ, as portrayed by the author of Mark's Gospel, is a tragic hero. First, he is abandoned by all his disciples, who scatter in fear when he is arrested.

Second, he is crucified, nailed to two pieces of crossed wood. Such Roman capital punishment was used to intimidate the Jews, whose country was occupied by the Romans. Crucifixion was done with abandon. A man was nailed through the wrists and through the feet to the wooden beams. He was stripped naked so that all his vulnerable parts could be poked and stabbed as he writhed in pain.

Third, Jesus feels abandoned by God. His final cry from the cross is a question of why has God left him. The hero of the gospel ends up dead. It is not the usual ending where all live happily ever after.

Jesus is the model of how a person handles tragedy. Even though he is abandoned by all his disciples and feels abandoned even by God, he goes to his death trusting that he is doing God's will. He believes that God will make sense out of such abandonment. And, of course, God does.

What God reveals is that God is present in tragedy. Indeed, this was a new revelation. Anyone who was abandoned by his disciples, crucified, and felt abandoned by God was considered cursed. God reverses this understanding. God is exactly revealed where people had predetermined God would not be—in abandonment on the cross.

This is the message for men today. When they experience tragedy, they are not alone. God is being revealed through the tragedy in their lives. It may be hard to see and to understand at the moment, but given time the light of God shines through like a rainbow that breaks through the clouds after a shower.

When a man is faced with the tragedy of the death of a friend, a spouse, or a child, he can begin to look for the face of God in death. God was revealed in the face of Jesus Christ in death on the cross.

When a man is faced with the tragedy of losing a job or not being able to find a new job, he can look for the face of God in his feeling of helplessness. God was revealed in the face of the helplessness of Jesus Christ hung naked on the cross.

Tragedy is a part of life. The Jesus of Mark's Gospel reveals that in moments of abandonment God is present. Indeed, heroic tragedy flashes forth from the God who reverses all of life—and death.

Meditation: What tragedy have you experienced in your life? Did you feel abandoned by God or others? How was God revealed in the tragic event of your life?

Prayer: God of Jesus Christ, you did not save your only-begotten Son from suffering and death, but revealed your presence in the moments of deepest abandonment. As I gaze upon the face of the crucified man of Nazareth, give me the wisdom to see your glory. Keep me faithful to him who lives and reigns with you and the Holy Spirit, one God, for ever and ever. Amen.

Index of Scripture Passages

Genesis
6:12-14, 16-22; 7:12, 17-18;
  8:3, 15-17; 9:8-15, pp. 19–20
18:1-14, pp. 9–10
22:1-13, 15-18, pp. 12–13
32:23-31, p. 16
39:1-6, p. 22

Exodus
3:1-8, 10; 4:10-14, 16,
  pp. 25–26
11:1-10, p. 28

Leviticus
8:1-15, 18-19, 22-24,
  pp. 31–32

Numbers
22:9-12; 24:2-13, pp. 34–35

Joshua
1:1-3, 5-11, p. 37

Judges
6:1-2, 11-16, 25-27; 7:2, 8,
  16-18, 21-22; 8:22-23, pp.
  39–40
13:2-5, 24; 15:4-5; 16:4-5, 17,
  19-25, 28-30, pp. 42–43

1 Samuel
3:1-18, pp. 45–46
17:55-58; 18:1-5; 19:1-10;
  20:1-4, 30-33, 35, 41-42;
  21:1, pp. 48–50

2 Samuel
5:1-3; 6:2, 12-15, 17-19;
  11:2-5, pp. 52–53

1 Kings
3:3-15, pp. 55–56
18:19-40, pp. 58–59
19:19-21, pp. 62–63

2 Kings
2:6, 8-14, pp. 62–63

Tobit
1:3-4, 6-13, 16-20, pp. 65–66

1 Maccabees
2:49, 66-67, 69; 3:1-2, 10-23,
  25-26, pp. 68–69

Job
1:1, 6-22, pp. 71–72

Isaiah
6:1-8, p. 74

108 *Biblical Reflections on Male Spirituality*

Jeremiah
1:4-10, p. 77

Ezekiel
2:1-6, 8-9; 3:1-9, pp. 80–81

Daniel
6:2-25, pp. 83–84

Hosea
1:1-8; 2:4-7, pp. 87–88

Jonah
1:1-16; 2:1, 11; 3:1-10,
  pp. 90–92

Matthew
3:1-12, p. 94

Mark
15:22-39, pp. 103–104

John
21:15-19, p. 97

Romans
1:1-7, p. 100

Hebrews
13:1, p. 11